Feeding the Young Athlete

Sports Nutrition Made Easy for Players and Parents

Cynthia Lair

with Scott Murdoch, PhD, RD

MOON SMILE PRESS

Copyright ©2002 Cynthia Lair and Scott Murdoch

Moon Smile Press
11038 27th Ave. NE
Seattle, WA 98125

Interior design by Joy Taylor
Illustrations by Cynthia Lair and Grace Geiger

Library of Congress Catalogue Card Number: 2002105392

Lair, Cynthia, 1953-
Murdoch PhD RD, Scott, 1960-
Feeding the Young Athlete:
Sports nutrition made easy for players and parents

ISBN: 0-9660346-9-4

The information in this book has been prepared thoughtfully and carefully. It is not intended to be diagnostic or prescriptive. Any child playing sports should have a regular physical examination from their health-care practitioner.

Dedicated to the FCA Gold '87.
The strength and beauty of these young women
has been inspiring to me.
— Cynthia

Dedicated to my wife, Pat, who constantly demonstrates
selfless acts of kindness and generosity, for which I have the
greatest love and admiration;
and my son, Hudson, who embodies the sheer magic of
movement with every step he takes,
reminding me of why I'm here.
— Scott

Acknowledgements

A deeply-felt thank you to the Geiger family, particularly Bill and Lura. Your respect and support have been invaluable.

Much appreciation to the fine coaches who let us work with their players — Steve Wilson and Steve Savory of FCA Momentum and Mark Osborne of FC Crunch.

Hats off to Jeff Basom, My-Duyen Huynh, Mary Shaw, Ronit Gourarie, Elena Leonard, Sandi Navarro, and Gay Stielstra who shared their culinary talents.

A big cheer for the team who put the book together: Michael Boer, Joy Taylor, Robin Lofstrom, and Paige Tyley.

Contents

Introduction

We believe that children need to move and be physically active for health, confidence, and well-being. For activity to be both healthy and enjoyable, children need to be well fed. Being physically active without eating wholesome foods, or eating wholesome foods without any activity is simply self-defeating.

There is a golden opportunity here! Educating young players and parents about the very popular topic of sports nutrition is a perfect way to both improve performance and to improve lifelong eating habits. Parents sometimes use sports events as yet another excuse to give their children junk food. Why not use the child's desire to participate in sports as an opportunity to teach the young athlete how food and the body work together?

There is a huge rise in the number of children participating in sports, yet there seems to be a dearth of available, easy-to-understand, practical information on the topic of sports nutrition for kids. Scott and I teach at Bastyr University, a school on the cutting edge of medicine and nutrition. The nutrition department combines the best of modern scientific research with the wisdom of emphasizing natural, whole foods. Using combined backgrounds in exercise physiology/sports nutrition and cooking/family food issues, we have created a practical, easy-to-read resource to fill this gap.

Although this booklet is directed at team sports, the information is applicable for individual sports such as swimming, track, and tennis.

By following our sports nutrition guidelines, it is reasonable that an individual athlete or a team can find a whole new level of play. Eating wisely and well increases energy, endurance, and the ability to concentrate. Players who eat and drink properly have an edge over their competition, especially in the second half of the game or at the second game of the day!

Eat better to play your best!

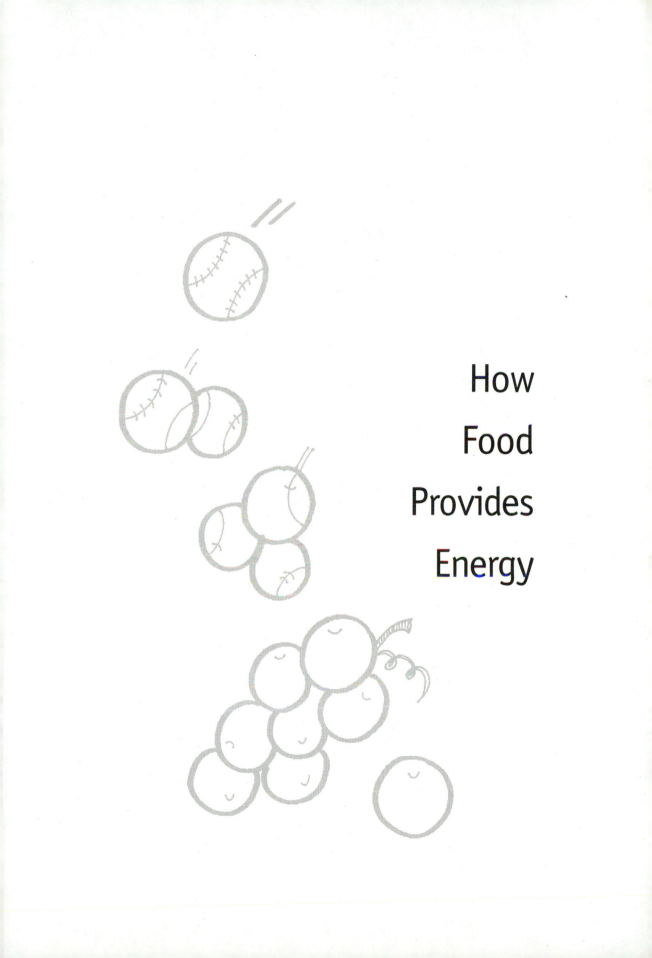

How
Food
Provides
Energy

Nutrients work together synergistically. Just as it is more effective to play basketball with a whole team rather than one player, nutrients work more efficiently when they are matched up with teammates. A good example is the nutrient calcium. If you take a pill that is 100% calcium and nothing else, that's okay. But if the calcium has the right amount of other important nutrients like magnesium and vitamin C with it, the calcium will perform at a higher level and your body will absorb more of the nutrient.

Who's on the team?

Foods naturally grow with a team of nutrients. The main nutritional components of every food are:

protein

carbohydrate

fat

vitamins (like Vitamin C, Vitamin D)

minerals (like calcium, iron)

fiber

water

Foods found in nature have some of each of these components in varying amounts. Fats help certain vitamins, like vitamin A, E, and K, to be better absorbed. The fiber helps keep the other nutrients flowing through all the tubes in your body. The carbohydrate in the food can provide your muscles with energy but it takes vitamins and minerals to transform the carbohydrate into fuel your muscles can use. The different types of nutrients help each other out, creating an unbeatable team.

Nature creates whole foods. That means that they don't have just one of the nutrients listed above, but a group of them. Whole foods are nutrient-dense. In other words, whole foods have a whole bunch of good players formed into a team, not just one lonely player. To figure out whether a food is a whole food or not, you just have to ask yourself if it was manufactured in a factory or grown in a field. Or better yet, read the label. If it's a whole food, you should be able to recognize every ingredient as something that grows in nature.

Without a doubt, the best foods for supporting an active human body are whole foods. Whole grains like oats, brown rice, corn, whole wheat, buckwheat, and quinoa are superb. The most nutrient-dense vegetables are the dark leafy green and orange vegetables like sweet potatoes, broccoli, collard greens, carrots and bok choy. Bananas, apples, strawberries, peaches, and melon are whole fruits that give us vitamins and energy and satisfy the sweet tooth. Beans, eggs, chicken, and fish are examples of other whole foods that emphasize protein but contain other valuable nutrients as well. Nuts and seeds, butter, yogurt, olives, and avocados are a few of the whole foods that combine healthy fats with important vitamins and minerals.

Best of all, when you put a few whole foods together, you can make some incredible things to eat. Like when you combine flour and water and yeast, top it with tomatoes, onions, peppers, mushrooms, and cheese, and make pizza! Or put together oats, nuts, honey, and apples to make apple crisp. Take a banana, some strawberries, yogurt and ice on a date to the blender and you have a smoothie! Very exciting.

Why are we told to eat carbs before a game?

When you eat a starchy food, like a banana, the carbohydrates are changed into blood sugar or glucose, which muscles burn for energy. Any glucose that's not immediately used gets stored in the muscles and liver as glycogen – which can be used for energy later. Glycogen is the preferred fuel for muscles.

All physical activities performed at a moderate to high intensity require glycogen as the primary energy source. Foods that contain mostly carbohydrates give your body this most important energy-providing fuel. To get some good play time out of the meal you eat before your game, the major portion of the meal should be carbohydrate-based. It's not surprising that most whole foods, foods that Nature creates, have ample carbohydrates.

Good sources of mostly carbohydrate foods are grains, vegetables, and fruits. That translates into oatmeal with fresh blueberries, or rice and stir-fried vegetables. There will be lots of examples later.

The catch is this: in order for the carbohydrates to make this magical transformation into muscle energy they require some teammates – vitamins and minerals. And the best place to get those? Fresh vegetables and fruit. Some protein is essential too. The amino acids which make up protein help stimulate the transformation of carbohydrates into muscle glycogen. So when you are planning your ultimate pre-game meal, put the carbohydrates on the starting line-up but don't forget to add fruits, vegetables, and a protein source as teammates.

Doesn't sugar give you quick energy?

Eating sugar gives most people a rush of very short-lived energy. The calories in high sugar products are empty or naked. That means they have no other nutrients associated with them, just carbohydrates. Products made with lots of sugar generally contain little protein, fat, fiber, water, vitamins or minerals… no teammates.

When you eat sugary foods or candy, your body needs the help of other important nutrients to process the sugar. Here's why. Sugar is refined to such a degree that it does not have to go through the normal slow digestive process – it goes right into your bloodstream. In most cases, this quick entry into the blood causes the glucose levels to increase, giving you a rush of frenetic energy. But this feeling of energy can be fleeting. The body then tries regain its balance of glucose and insulin. To accomplish this the body uses important nutrients like B vitamins, calcium, phosphorus, iron, chromium, zinc and manganese. Interestingly, these are all nutrients associated with healthy mental and emotional functioning and good bone health. What could be more vital to the young athlete than excellent concentration, steady composure, and strong bones? Yet many kids come to games fueled up on sugary cereals or snack foods. And the most common post-game snacks given to young athletes are sugary foods like donuts, candy bars, and Twinkies. Perplexing. At a time when the body is in need of replenishment, young players are given foods that can ultimately deplete them further.

Young athletes need a steady source of fuel to get them through an athletic event as well as the other "events" taking place in their daily lives. And although sugary food can provide a quick jolt of energy, the true biological cost isn't justified. Complex carbohydrates found in grains, breads, pastas, and vegetables provide more of what the athlete needs.

Skip the protein and just go for the carbs?

NO WAY! Protein is what makes muscles grow. It makes hair grow and cells grow and everything grow to get stronger and more efficient. Protein also helps your body convert carbohydrates into the type of energy your muscles prefer for fuel. So no way do you want to leave out the protein as part of your sports nutrition program. For pre- and post-game meals however, you want to have carbohydrates and foods rich in vitamins and minerals be the leading nutrients. Protein and fat should be there in smaller proportion. Translation: a lot of rice and vegetables, with some teriyaki chicken strips thrown in.

Is low-fat/no-fat the way to go?

Not a chance! Remember how those nutrients work together? You need fat so you can utilize important vitamins and minerals, stay warm, protect your cells and organs and have nice hair and skin. Fats are in foods for another reason – they help the food taste better. No question that whole milk yogurt has a richer, creamier, more satisfying flavor than its non-fat counterpart. Yet we've been led to believe that we are being "good" by choosing the container with less fat. Not necessarily so. You'll eat less and be more satisfied with the food that hasn't had its natural fat removed by manufacturing.

The trick is, you want to eat healthful fats. How do you tell a healthful fat from a non-healthful fat? You have to be a bit of a detective. Some experts believe that the chemically manipulated fats and fats that have been exposed to extreme heat, light, and air (causing rancidity) are at fault for causing a myriad of disease problems in the body. Most processed foods contain these undesirable fats and oils. Avoid products whose labels include terms like "partially hydrogenated," "hydrogenated," "trans-fatty acids" or "refined oils." Healthy fats come from minimally processed whole foods such as unroasted nuts and seeds, fish, avocados, butter, and extra-virgin olive oil.

Although healthful fats are excellent for your body, loading up on fatty foods right before a game won't serve you well. Your body can't transform the fat into usable energy quickly and the fatty meal will send all your bodily forces towards a long slow digestion rather than to the muscles you need to get on base. So have a little butter on your bagel or pancake for your pre-game meal, but don't choose the double cheeseburger.

What are good sources of vitamins and minerals?

All whole foods, all foods found in nature, have some vitamins and minerals. It takes lots of processing and refining in a factory to strip a food of its natural vitamins and minerals. Yet many of the products on our grocery store shelves are canned, boxed, frozen, lifeless foods that have been robbed of these vital nutrients. Walk on by. Set your sights on the produce aisle. The most reliable sources of vitamins and minerals are fresh vegetables and fruit. These foods are the movers and the shakers. They give you the nutrients you need to transform carbohydrates, proteins and fats into usable energy. Fresh vegetables and fruit also have components called enzymes that aid in the digestion of all the other foods you eat with them. Thirty-five percent of the carbohydrates you eat for your pre-game meal should be from vegetables and fruit. Don't leave home without them. Athletes need to pay heed to the "5-a-day" credo. At least five servings of fresh vegetables and fruit every day, 7 days a week, 365 days a year.

What and
When to Feed
the Young Athlete

Eat Better to Play Your Best

Why is the pre-game meal important?

Inside each of our muscle fibers lives stored glycogen which gives the muscle fuel to use. Muscles can only store a limited amount of glycogen, so we must constantly replenish our stores by eating. When our glycogen levels are low we become slower, weaker and less able to concentrate. Glycogen is made from the food we eat, particularly carbohydrate-containing foods, so it is critical to eat a healthy meal containing ample carbohydrates prior to the game to have the muscle energy needed to play. As discussed earlier, the meal closest to game time needs to have most of its calories come from carbohydrates because they convert into energy quicker and more efficiently than other nutrients. It is also important to include a source of vitamins and minerals with the pre-game meal to help the body transform carbohydrates into energy.

If you come to a game or a scrimmage without having eaten you will not have the energy or concentration to play at your full potential. Some players try to down a bagel or toast a half hour before the game because they have forgotten to eat earlier. If you do this, your body's primary focus during the first half of the game will be on digesting that food. You won't have given your body time to transform the food into energy the muscles can use.

Never come to a game, practice, or scrimmage without fuel in your tank! When is game time? Your pre-game meal should be eaten about **2 to 3 hours before** your game, practice, or scrimmage. For good, long-lasting energy the meal should consist of mostly whole grains, cereals, pastas, or breads accompanied by a fruit or vegetable and some protein. Eat until full, but don't stuff yourself.

WHEN TO DRINK

2-3 hours before   Drink fluids (2-3 cups). See page 21.

1-2 hours before   Drink fluids (½ - 1 cup).

1 hour before   Drink fluids (½ -1 cup).

Game or training   Drink fluids (½ -1 cup).

0-1 hour after   Drink fluids (2-3 cups).

Smaller amounts are for younger players, more for teens.

WHEN TO EAT

Pre-Game Meal (2-3 hours before)
Pasta, rice, bread, potatoes, veggies or fruit; plus some protein. See list on page 12.

Pre-Game Snack (1 hour before)

Very light fare, only if needed. Fresh fruit, crackers, bread. See list on page 15.

0-1 hour before

No food

Game or training

No food

Post-Game Snack (within 1 hour)

100% fruit juices, fresh fruit, bagel, muffin, sandwich, crackers, energy bars. See list on page 27.

PRE-GAME MEAL SUGGESTIONS

Look at High Performance Recipes (pages 46-88) for more ideas!

Breakfast

Cream of wheat with fresh blueberries
French toast and orange juice
Granola (page 51) and milk or yogurt and ½ grapefruit
Hash browns and scrambled eggs
Huevos Rancheros
Oatmeal (page 92) with raisins or bananas and milk
Pancakes or waffles (pages 50, 52, 94) and fruit salad
Yogurt and fresh fruit (page 83) with a muffin

Lunch/Dinner

Bagel and lox sandwich and lemonade (page 48)
Baked potato with vegetable and sour cream toppings
Black bean soup (page 70) and quesadillas (page 71)
Chicken noodle soup (page 54) and apple slices
Fish Tacos (page 74-75)
Fried rice (pages 72) with shrimp and steamed broccoli
Lentil soup and spinach salad (page 59)
Macaroni and cheese, carrots and celery, applesauce
Mashed potatoes (page 65), salad and baked chicken
Minestrone soup (page 56) and turkey sandwich
Moo Shu vegetables with rice
Nori rolls or sushi (pages 80-81)
Pesto pasta (page 79) and salad (page 59)
Phad Thai
Pita bread and hummus with fresh vegetables
Rice and bean burrito
Roasted potatoes, green beans and grilled salmon
Sesame noodles (page 64) with chicken and vegetables
Spaghetti with vegetable marinara sauce
Tabouli with chickpeas
Tomato soup and a peanut butter sandwich
Tuna sandwich and a fruit smoothie (page 48)
Vegetarian chili and cornbread (page 69)
Chicken and vegetable teriyaki over rice (page 78)

PRE-GAME MEAL PLATE

Here's what your pre-game meal plate should look like:

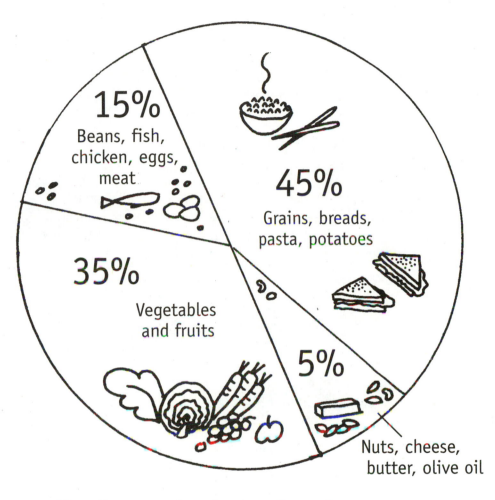

15% Beans, fish, chicken, eggs, meat

45% Grains, breads, pasta, potatoes

35% Vegetables and fruits

5% Nuts, cheese, butter, olive oil

Note: Percentages by volume, not by weight.
This chart was designed to prepare the young athlete
for practice and competition. It is not intended to
reflect what a growing child's overall diet should
look like.

Away from home?

Look for these grocery store foods or restaurants for your Pre-Game Meal:

Bean burritos, fish or chicken tacos
Chinese or Thai food
Deli sandwiches or pasta dishes
Japanese food
Hero sandwich
Wrapped sandwiches (vegetables, rice, beans, etc., wrapped in flour tortillas)

How do I eat for an early morning game?

· Eat an excellent dinner the night before

Include large portions of grains or pasta, vegetables and small to medium portions of beans, chicken, fish, or meat. (see Pre-Game Meal Plate, page 13 and Pre-Game Meal Suggestions, page 12)

· Have a snack an hour before going to bed

Not usually recommended but in this case could be helpful. No candy, soda, or ice cream the night before competition.
popcorn
tortilla chips and salsa
crackers and cheese
oatmeal cookie (page 87)
fruit smoothie (page 48)

· 1-2 hours before the game have a pre-game snack/mini breakfast

This pre-game snack is very important!

Bagel, muffin, scone, or toast (not a sweet roll or doughnut)
Small amount of yogurt and/or a piece of fruit
Big glass of water

PRE-GAME SNACKS

The *When to Drink, When to Eat* chart (page 11) says to have a pre-game snack "if needed." To tell whether you might need a pre-game snack or not, ask these questions:

1. Do I frequently run out of energy during the second half of a game or practice?

2. Do I have a quick metabolism – meaning do I feel the need to eat small amounts of food often?

3. Do I often not eat enough food for my pre-game meal? For example, a bowl of cold cereal with milk at 10:00 won't give you enough calories to sustain energy through your 1:00 game.

If any of these apply to you, try having an easily digestible snack one hour prior to a practice. If it works in practice and you discover your energy is better during the second half of practice, try a snack an hour before a game.

Suggestions:

100% fruit juice
Bagel
Bread
Crackers
Diluted sports drink (see page 21)
Dried fruit
Energy bar (see page 23)
Fresh fruit
Fresh vegetables
Raisin bread
Rice cakes
Smoothie
Yogurt

Are half-time snacks OK?

Young players have smaller bodies and sometimes they can't pack in enough food before a game to last them until the final whistle blows. Generally no food is recommended for the hour preceding and during the game. If you're working with players that fall into any or all of these categories you may want to consider a half-time snack.

• under 8 years of age

• have a quick metabolism

• tend to drag during the second half of the game

The best choice is a fruit with high water content – oranges, melons, grapes. This will give the player some fast-acting carbohydrate and also help re-hydrate them.

It is very important to try out the half-time snack at a practice. Don't try a new food plan for the first time at a game. Bring some juicy fruit to practice and have the player eat it during the break. Then watch and see if it is helpful or not. Ask the player if they felt their energy got stronger. If it did, and they "stomached" it well, then you can try the half-time snack at the next game.

Is eating before practice important?

Many parents and players get serious about eating and drinking well when a game or competition is at stake. It is equally important to remember to hydrate and feed the young athlete before and after every practice or training session. Often practices are held during the after school hours. Most children have not eaten since lunchtime and will need a hearty snack or mini-meal and water before heading out the door. A tired or lethargic child will not benefit from practice, and the coach and teammates won't benefit from a tired player. Offer fresh fruit, bagels, smoothies, sandwiches and, of course, water. Pack an extra banana, juice boxes, crackers or muffins in your child's back pack or sports bag. Carry some granola, apples, dried fruit and water in the car. Keep young athletes well-fed so they can have fun and learn at practice.

POOR CHOICES FOR PRE- OR POST-GAME MEALS

It is best to forego high fat, high sugar foods prior to practice or competition. Foods high in fat will not leave the stomach or metabolize quickly enough to give you energy. Foods that contain a lot of sugar or caffeine will give you an initial rush of energy followed by sluggishness or irritability – not good qualities for game playing. Caffeine also causes frequent urination which contributes to dehydration, and can irritate the stomach lining.

Take care to avoid these foods before or after a game or event:

Anything with MSG

Caffeine: chocolate, coffee, latte, cola, frappucino

Candy

Cheeseburgers, hamburgers

Doughnuts and pastries

French fries

Fried chicken or fried fish sandwiches

Fructose, high fructose, high fructose corn syrup

Highly sugared, refined cereals (like Fruit Loops)

Milkshakes and ice cream

Pepperoni pizza with double cheese

Soda pop

Wet Your Whistle

Why is hydration so important?

The sports water bottle is standard gear for every young player going to a game or practice. But are they actually drinking the water? Why are they supposed to drink and how much is enough? When should they drink? Before the game, after, or both? Is water the only choice?

The reason young athletes need to stay hydrated during play is physiological. When a child plays hard his or her body temperature elevates. Kid's bodies don't regulate body temperature as well as adults. One reason is that pre-pubescent children do not sweat as much as adults because their sweat glands are not fully developed. Small children have a larger surface area to mass ratio. This heightens their metabolic heat production and also causes them to absorb more heat from the outside in hotter climates and lose heat faster in colder weather.

If the body is not well-hydrated, energy will go to regulating temperature instead of to the muscles, and limits playing ability. The body will steal water from inside the cells in order to cool itself which limits muscle function. Allowed to continue, the player can suffer symptoms of heat exhaustion (dizziness, nausea, profuse sweating) or heatstroke (hot dry skin, headaches, rapid pulse, faintness, flushing) and/or muscle cramps. For this reason parental monitoring of fluid intake becomes crucial during events held in hot weather. The second most common sports injury among young players, yet also the most preventable, is heat exhaustion or heat stroke which is usually complicated by dehydration.

When we exercise, our bodies produce waste that the kidneys and liver must work to eliminate. Drinking water after play helps the body flush out waste so that recovery is quicker. Without appropriate amounts of liquid, players may feel more sluggish and tired after an event. This can become quite a hindrance during tournaments when there is more than one game or event per day.

When and how much should I drink?

The following are general guidelines. Some players may require more water, some a bit less. Hydration is more crucial in a strenuous game like soccer than it is for a more leisurely sport. And climate must be considered. Hot weather (or even a hot gym!) will demand more frequent hydration.

Hydration needs to begin before competition. An hour or two before a game or practice, the player needs to start drinking water. It's actually more effective to sip water than to chug it down. If the player downs two cups of water at one sitting, they may end up with a sloshing belly and be too bloated to play. Two cups spread out over an hour and a half is a good amount. One way to accomplish this task is to drink a glass of water before eating the pre-game meal. Another way is to sip from a water bottle in the car on the way to the game. We keep a case of water bottles by the door so that grabbing one on the way to the car is easy to remember.

Parents should continue to encourage drinking sips of water before the game. This is very important when playing in hot weather. Often players are nervous, busy practicing drills, or just being silly with the energy of having friends and team mates around, and forget to drink. If you feel you are becoming a nag or compliance is low, get another parent or the coach to give drinking instructions. Sometimes kids will follow orders from anyone but their parents.

During the event, or during time-outs and half-times, encourage players to continue sipping. Give clear, specific instructions like, "You need to drink 10 sips of water before you go back out to play." Parents need to make sure there is always water available so that the player who forgets their water bottle or whose water bottle is empty does not go without. Perhaps one parent on the team can be designated to bring water to every game. Sometimes during strenuous exercise the player's sense of thirst is not engaged, yet the body needs water to regulate body temperature and remove waste. Let kids know that it is important to drink even if they don't feel thirsty.

Handing players cups of water or diluted juice after the game is one way of assuring post-game hydration. Often drinking will begin without thinking and the mission is accomplished. Parents and coachs can set a good example by bringing a water bottle and drinking frequently.

Each player should bring a liter of water to every game and make sure it is ½ empty by the time the game starts. Notice that we suggest at least ½ cup of fluids at half-time. Pour out a half-cup and count how many sips it takes to drink all of it. Then the player knows exactly how much to drink at half time. Several girls on our team counted how many sips it took finish this amount. It took one player 10 sips to finish ½ cup and another only 7. Parents and coaches can be very helpful by calling out things like: "Drink 10 sips before you go back in." "Eight big swigs and then let's talk about the second half."

Sports nutrition research teaches us that the proper amount of water to consume can be calculated. It is suggested that the player weigh themselves before the practice/event and after. Sixteen ounces of fluid should be consumed for every pound of body weight lost. The problem with applying this test to children is practicality, consistency, and compliance. The logistics of weighing a child before and after an event are awkward. Plus the results will only be accurate for the temperature of that day's play and will change again if the game is played in a hotter or cooler environment. The results will also change each time your child has a growth spurt and as they begin to show signs of puberty. Another slightly less accurate way to gauge how much water needs to be consumed is by having player's check their urine – when it runs clear, the player is adequately hydrated.The coach's or parent's advice for players is to "drink until you pee clear." For players who are serious about priming their body for an event, these hydration tests can provide important feedback.

What's best to drink?

Water is the best. Some studies show that the presence of flavoring in a beverage enhances thirst and increases voluntary hydration. If you choose to provide electrolytic-based drinks, dilute them by one half to increase their effectiveness. You can get all of the flavoring and sodium you need with half the amount. The most important factor in the drink is the water. Simply adding a little lemon, or lemon and a teaspoon of honey or sugar, to water can be a much less expensive way of stimulating drinking. Bringing a container of diluted lemonade or limeade can be an appealing way to encourage hydration. Liquids should be should be 59-72° F (cool, not cold).

Yes

• Water
• Water flavored with citrus or other fruit
• Diluted lemonade, limeade or other 100% fruit juice
• Sports drinks (see page 23)

No

Do not use the following beverages, or beverages that contain these ingredients, to hydrate children before, during or after athletic events:

• Carbonated drinks
• Unfiltered apple juice
• Caffeinated beverages
• High fructose corn syrup, fructose, corn syrup

Carbonated drinks change the pH levels in the stomach and can produce belching and gas. Unfiltered apple juice can cause stomach cramping in some players. Caffeinated beverages act as a diuretic which is not helpful when the goal is to rehydrate. They also can cause nervousness and shaking in some people. High fructose corn syrup, fructose and corn syrup are highly refined sweeteners that are unable to be fully utilized by the human body. They become waste for the body to dispose of and are sent to the intestines where water is needed in order to pass the substance. In other words, foods and liquids containing these chemical sweeteners can contribute to dehydration! These sweeteners are also known to cause cramping, bloating, and sometimes diarrhea.

What if I'm not thirsty?

Hydration is about more than being thirsty. You need to drink to regulate body temperature, hydrate muscle cells, and remove waste. Carry at least 1 liter of water or other acceptable fluids to every practice and game. (1 liter = a little over 4 cups or 1 quart.)

Get into the habit of drinking small amounts frequently rather than chugging water right before you play. If you have to travel to get to your game or practice, sip fluids in the car on the way. Remember to take a few sips before starting your warm up and every time you take a break. Don't forget to drink again when the practice or event is over. For specific amounts see page 11. Sipping fluids throughout the day will insure that your body is well-hydrated, ready to perform and able to recover.

SHOPPING FOR SPORTS BARS AND FLUIDS

	Better Choices	**OK Choices**
Bars	ReBar	Harvest Power Bar
	Boulder Bar	Luna Bar
	Odwalla Bar	Cliff Bar
	Real Food Bar	
Drinks	Water	Propel
	Knudsen's Recharge	Gatorade Ice
	Diluted organic	100% fruit juices
	100% fruit juices	
Other	Organic fig bars	Gels & Gu
	VigorAid (liquid meal)	Organic cookies
	Organic yogurt	Yogurt

© 2002 C. Lair and S. Murdoch

Criteria* for Rating the Quality of Foods and Drinks

1. Ingredients are food-based
   (not isolated nutrients/compounds)   4 points
2. Ingredients are from organically grown foods   3 points
3. Generally higher in carbohydrates, lower in fat
   and variable protein   1 point
4. Overall convenience
   (e.g., packaging, keeps at room temperature)   1 point
5. Does not contain any potent drug-like nutrients
   (e.g., caffeine)   1 point

Total: 10 points

*Although we recognize that taste has a powerful influence on food choice, we do not include it as a criterion due to its high degree of subjectivity.

Replenish and Come Back Stronger

How does post-game/post-practice eating help?

During exercise your body uses up stored energy in the form of muscle glycogen. The body also produces waste and stress hormones that need to be flushed out and creates tiny microtears in muscle tissue that needs to be repaired. To recover after exercise, players need to drink fluids, eat and relax. If athletes don't focus some attention on recovery, their overall progress is slowed down. When players do take time to restore fluids, replenish food, stretch and rest – they can come back stronger the next day.

Research has shown that our muscles are able to replenish their glycogen needs more quickly when we eat or drink carbohydrate-containing foods within the first 30 minutes after a game or practice. During this time muscles will convert carbohydrates into glycogen up to three times faster than if the player waits until two hours after the game to eat. There are two explanations for this phenomenon:

1. Increased blood flow to the muscle cells brings more nutrients to make glycogen.

2. The muscle cells are more sensitive to the substances that transform nutrients into glycogen immediately after play.

Which brings up another key point in recovery research – the importance of including a small amount of protein in the post-game snack or meal. The best ratio is one part protein per four parts carbohydrate (this 1:4 ratio has been shown effective for adults; no research has been done testing children). The protein stimulates insulin which helps glucose transform into muscle glycogen.

The bottom line: eat healthy carbohydrate-containing snacks and beverages as soon as you can after the game or practice is finished. This snack or meal is extremely important if players have another game, scrimmage or practice within 12-24 hours. Ideally, if the players have a second game the same day they will have a nutritious snack immediately after the game followed by a more substantial meal.

What should I eat after the game?

Make-up of the post-game meal or snack should mirror the formula for the pre-game meal only using smaller portions. Ideally players will want to consume lots of fluids (see "Yes" list on page 21) and a carbohydrate-rich snack that also has some protein value. Think appetizers – like serving players a big plate of fresh fruit, crackers or bread, and cheese. Our team gobbles down mini-sandwiches – like a turkey or tuna sandwich cut into fourths. Remember to chew! Don't wolf down food. Your stomach will have to do the work if your teeth don't. More suggestions follow.

Don't kids deserve a treat for working so hard?

We have a strange notion in our culture that if you've worked really hard, you deserve a big, gooey, sugary dessert. Maybe that satisfies some emotional longing but it is certainly not what growing young bodies need for recovery. Using the completion of a game as yet another excuse to give kids pop, candy, doughnuts and junk food sends the wrong message to the head and the wrong food to the body. Be clear. What the body needs is some real, wholesome food. What the head and heart need is a lot of positive comments about the game that was just played.

Do players need specially formulated recovery drinks?

Most nutritionists would say this is unnecessary. These pre-formulated drinks may be convenient but they are very expensive. Plus you won't necessarily get more or better nutrients fom these drinks than you would from an apple, some grape juice, or a bagel sandwich. Your local grocery store should have everything the young athlete needs.

What if I miss the glycogen window?

Circumstances don't always allow for optimal sports nutrition. If someone forgot to bring snacks or there's no time to stop and get something to eat, don't panic. Recovery is attainable later, it's just that the body is more efficient at resupplying immediately after the event.

Another thing to remember is that calories of any kind consumed post game are better than no calories consumed.

When players pack their sports bags for the game, be sure to include a piece of fruit or some crackers – some kind of snack. Make it part of the pre-game ritual before you leave the house. That way you'll be less likely to miss the glycogen window.

What is the two-week slump?

If players keep up a high intake of healthy carbohydrate foods, paying heed to pre-game and post-game eating opportunities, their performance level will at the very least remain stable. Players that pay less attention to what and when they eat will not experience similar results. At the beginning of the training or playing season, energy and performance levels may seem okay, but studies and experience show there will be a notable decline in performance at or shortly after two weeks. This decline is particularly noticeable in players who have been eating a low-carbohydrate diet or who aren't consuming enough calories day after day.

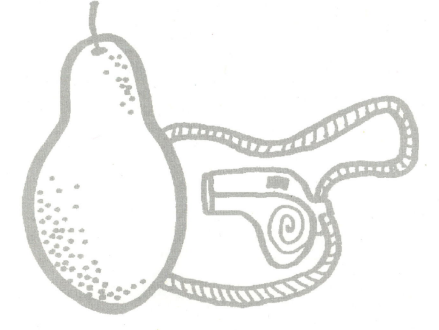

POST-GAME SNACK SUGGESTIONS

Fluids:

100% fruit juices, water, sports drinks (page 23)
Lemonade (page 48)
Smoothie (page 48)

Foods:

Apples
Bananas
Grapes
Melon slices
Oranges
Strawberries

Bagels
Bagels with butter or spread
Banana bread (page 84)
Corn bread (page 69)
Crackers, fresh fruit, and cheese
Fig bars
Fresh vegetables and dip
Graham crackers
Granola (page 51)
Half sandwiches
Muffins
Oatmeal cookies (page 87)
Pasta or noodles
Pita bread and hummus
Quesadillas (page 71)
Raisin bread
Raspberry Pecan Bars (page 85)
Rice or potatoes
Sushi Rolls (pages 80-81)
Tortilla chips and bean dip or salsa
Rice cakes with spreads
Yogurt (pages 28, 83)

BRAND NAMES TO LOOK FOR

Always read labels!

Juices or juice drinks

These companies make juices or juice drink products that contain mostly juice and that don't contain fructose, corn syrup, high fructose corn syrup, or aspartame (Nutra Sweet).

Columbia Gorge	Mountain Sun
Crystal Geyser	Nantucket Nectar
Dole	Natural Brew
Horizon	Odwalla
Knudsens	Santa Cruz
Martinelli's	Viva Tierra
Minute Maid	

Yogurts

These brands aren't highly sugared or sweetened with fructose or other chemical sweeteners and they do contain live cultures.

Brown Cow
Cascade Fresh
Horizon
Nancy's
Stonyfield Farm

Crackers, Chips

These companies make crackers and chips that are whole-grain based.

Ak Mak	Lundburg
Barbara's	Newman's Own
Bearitos	Que Pasa
Garden of Eatin'	Ryvita
Hain Health Valley	Wasa
Hol Grain	Westbrae
Kettle	

Why is ice magical?

When a player is injured it is important to put ice on the injury right away. The ice keeps the area from swelling. If the injured body part swells, the fluid restricts the area and the player will have a considerable decrease in mobility. The sooner the ice is put on the injured area, the more efficiently it works. The process of icing brings fresh blood to the area in the body's effort to stay warm. This movement of blood helps carry off injured cells and replaces them with new cells which accelerates the healing process.

The reusable cold packs you buy at the drug store may be comforting to the injured player but they are not cold enough to perform the magic that a real ice compress can.

Have someone on your team bring ice to every game. Buy one of those little coolers, the type that just holds a six-pack. They come with a hard or soft shell – either one is fine. Take a one gallon zip-lock plastic bag and fill it half full with ice. Press the air out, seal it, and fold the top half over. Now, put a second zip-lock bag over it and repeat the sealing process. The second bag keeps the ice pack from leaking, which can be messy and uncomfortable. It's a good idea to pack two or three of these zip-lock ice packs in your cooler in case there's more than one injury. This becomes especially important if your team is in the latter half of a series of games where injuries are more likely, due to tiredness. You'll also need to pack some sort of long cloth, rag, or scarf. We find that a winter scarf is long enough and sturdy enough to work well; large bandanas also do the job. Shrink wrap is excellent for holding ice packs in place on injured body parts.

When the injured player comes off the field place a wet towel over the affected area. Then put one of your ice packs on the towel. Tie the cloth or scarf or wrap the shrink wrap around the pack and the injured body part so that the ice is compressed against the painful area.

Without the compression, the ice will not work as effectively. Don't expect an upset child to dutifully hold the ice on the injury with the amount of pressure it will take to make it work. Wrap the ice securely and keep it on the player for 15-30 minutes. Repeat the icing every 1-2 hours for the next 48-72 hours or until the swelling has been controlled.

Another useful product to have in your injury first aid kit is arnica cream. Arnica is a natural substance used in the treatment of bruises, sprains and muscle pain. If I remember to apply arnica right away to my child's bruised shin, the skin won't even turn purple. Several companies make creams with arnica in them. You might want to keep a tube in your child's sports bag. Rub some on the injured area between icings.

Here's another magical way to use ice. When the weather is really hot, players can get over-heated which can lead to heat exhaustion. The quickest way to bring the body temperature down is by wrapping an icy cloth or towel around the back of the neck. Bring bandanas and ice to hot weather games. Put a little crushed ice in the center of the bandana and roll it up. Tie the ice bandage around the hot player's neck when they come off the field. Another option is to put a bunch of small towels in a bucket and fill the bucket with ice. Offer icy towels for the necks of flushed young players.

Getting the
Whole Team
Involved

How can everyone benefit from better eating?

When all the players on a team are educated about the importance of feeding oneself properly for hard play, it affects the whole tone of the team. The concentration and endurance of the team will increase. If each player is dedicated to utilizing good sports nutrition it adds to team morale. Having common rituals and goals brings the team together making it a "whole" rather than a group of individuals.

Not only will the team's play improve, each player can learn something valuable about the connection between how we eat and how fit our bodies are. It is ineffective to talk to a child about what they eat today and how it may lead to a heart condition when they are in their fifties. For a child, that is too far away to imagine. But if you talk about how their meal this morning will affect their game this afternoon, the benefits are immediate and they're more likely to be interested.

There is an obvious benefit for parents as well. Some children develop poor eating habits despite ceaseless efforts from their parents. Moms and dads may see new hope, even dramatic changes, when information about good eating comes from coaches or trainers, peer pressure from teammates, or simply a genuine desire to improve athletic performance.

How can I get the whole team on board?

A coach, team manager, or an enthusiastic parent can set aside time at a player/parent meeting to talk to everyone about feeding young bodies so they're fit to play. Some teams may even be willing to dedicate a whole meeting to the subject followed by a social event. Make the talk on sports nutrition fun and engaging. We have players fill out a pre-game meal survey like the one on page 34. By doing this the players must take time to read a list of appropriate pre-game meals and then they get to exert their individuality by choosing preferences. The results can be valuable information for parents and players. We posted

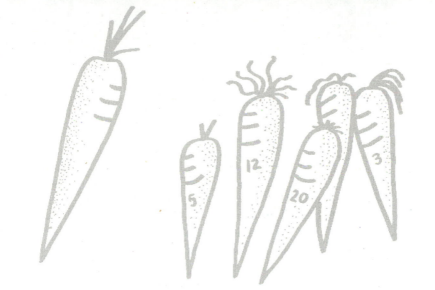

the team's top five favorite meals on our web site. Bringing in different drinks and foods and letting players do "taste tests" is another way of generating fun and interest, as well as respecting the players' opinions.

Parents assigned (or who volunteer) to organize team snacks can be very instrumental in generating good sports nutrition habits. Along with assigning families to bring snacks to different games, the snack organizer can create a list of great snack ideas with a few notes on which foods to avoid serving to tired athletes.

Coaches can be very influential. They certainly need to remind players to stay hydrated before, during, and after games, but they can also remind players to eat a good meal before coming to practices or games. Not only will the health of the players improve, so will their performance. Making sure players participate in good sports nutrition eating habits can also help prevent injury. The fatigued player who is losing concentration is more likely to get injured.

One of the most entertaining ways to emphasize good sports nutrition habits is to plan some team meals. We used to have a big team breakfast before the 1-2 hour car ride to out of town games. Not only did this assure that everyone was well fed, the team entered the event with a sense of support and camaraderie. Team meals can also be organized for the night before a big game. Ideas for team meals are on pages 36-37.

OUR TEAM'S PRE-GAME MEAL SURVEY

Name:_____

*Put a number in front of 8 pre-game meals that sound
good to you, with number 1 as your most favorite and
number 8 less favorite. If you can't find 8 you like, invent
a pre-game meal that you think would taste good and give
you good energy and write it down in one of the blank spaces.*

_____ Cream of wheat with fresh blueberries

_____ French toast and orange juice

_____ Granola and milk or yogurt and ½ grapefruit

_____ Hash browns and scrambled eggs

_____ Oatmeal with raisins or bananas and milk

_____ Pancakes or waffles and fruit salad

_____ Yogurt and fresh fruit with a muffin

_____ Bagel and lox sandwich

_____ Baked potato with sour cream and vegetable

_____ Black bean soup and quesadillas

_____ Chicken noodle soup and apple slices

_____ Fried rice with shrimp and steamed broccoli

_____ Macaroni and cheese, carrots and celery, applesauce

_____ Mashed potatoes, salad and baked chicken

_____ Minestrone soup and turkey sandwich

_____ Nori rolls or sushi

_____ Pesto pasta and salad

_____ Pita bread and hummus with fresh vegetables

_____ Rice and bean burrito

_____ Roasted potatoes, green beans and grilled salmon

_____ Sesame noodles with chicken and vegetables

_____ Spaghetti with vegetable marinara sauce

_____ Tomato soup and a peanut butter sandwich

_____ Tuna sandwich and a fruit smoothie

_____ Vegetarian chili and cornbread

Other ideas?

_____ _____

_____ _____

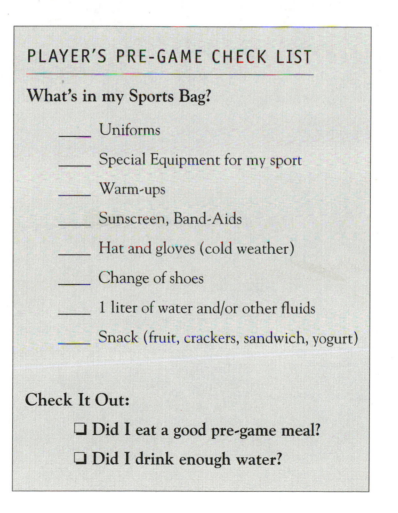

PLAYER'S PRE-GAME CHECK LIST

What's in my Sports Bag?

_____ Uniforms

_____ Special Equipment for my sport

_____ Warm-ups

_____ Sunscreen, Band-Aids

_____ Hat and gloves (cold weather)

_____ Change of shoes

_____ 1 liter of water and/or other fluids

_____ Snack (fruit, crackers, sandwich, yogurt)

Check It Out:

❏ Did I eat a good pre-game meal?

❏ Did I drink enough water?

IDEAS FOR TEAM MEALS

Rise, Shine, and Score Pancake Feast:

Pancakes, hash browns, scrambled eggs, toast and fresh
orange juice. Great for an early morning get together
before the drive to a big game.

Play Hard Pastamania:

Have several families bring their favorite pasta dishes
and a copy of the recipe used. Encourage pasta dishes
that include vegetables and some form of protein. Other
parents can bring green salads and beverages to round
out the meal.

Baffle the Opponent Baked Potato Spread:

Someone will need to bake a whole bunch of potatoes.
Add to that all kinds of condiments like cheddar cheese,
steamed broccoli, chopped scallions, fresh chives, tuna
salad, sour cream, chickpeas – let the ideas for toppings
roll.

We Got Mo Mexican Fiesta:

Tortillas, salsa, black beans, rice, cheese, olives,
guacamole, grilled chicken strips, refried pinto beans,
shredded lettuce dressed with lime vinaigrette – all set
up for a "build your own burrito" meal.

The Spaghetti Advantage:

Lots of spaghetti with several types of sauces – fresh
vegetables, simple marinara, red-wine, and mushrooms.
Add warm garlic bread and a huge tossed salad and
players will be fueled up fine.

Take Action Rice and Kabobs:

Use rice cookers to make mounds of brown and white
rice. Then offer plenty of big chunks of vegetables like
zucchini, portobello mushrooms, green and red peppers,
onions, plus pieces of skinless chicken breasts or

marinated tofu, and let players and parents make their own kabobs to slide over a bed of rice.

Power Up Bagels and Fruit:

How about a simple no-cooking-involved team meal? Lay out a big variety of bagels and spreads (there are so many besides just cream cheese on the market now). Side the bagels up with bowls of freshly sliced fruit or have a parent ride the blender churning out a few pitchers of fresh fruit smoothies.

On Your Mark Hot Soup and Fresh Bread:

Get several parents who like to cook to make their favorite soups. Minestrone, black bean, mushroom, lentil, tomato, chicken noodle – most kids are pleased to have a bowl of homemade soup. Buy several loaves of fresh, hearth breads, cut the slices thick, and warm the bread in the oven. There's nothing quite as nourishing as simple soup and bread.

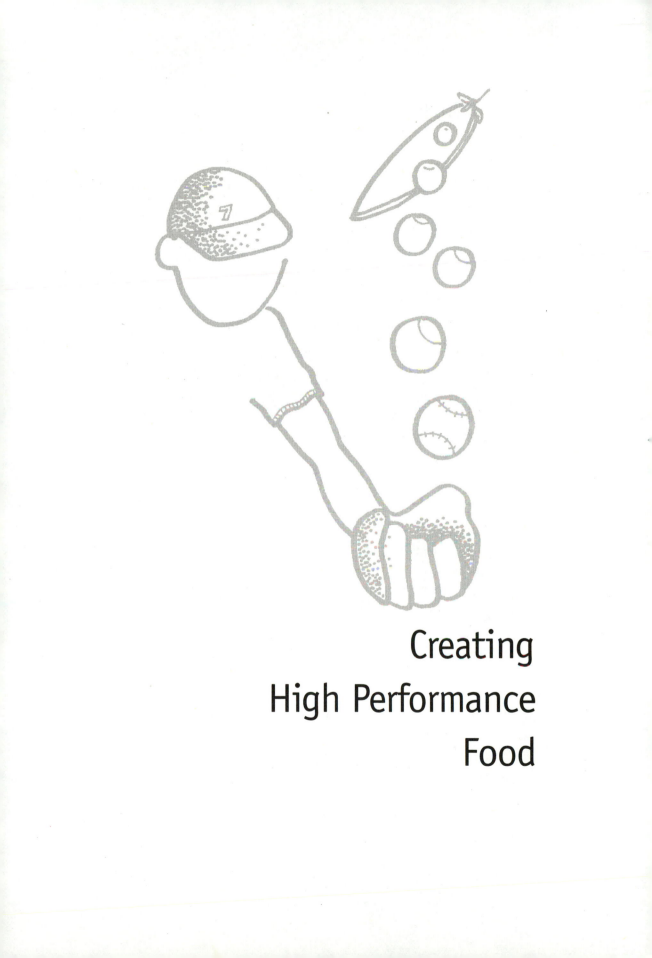

Creating
High Performance
Food

High Performance Food

The highest quality foods will yield the highest quality athletic performance. Under each category of food we've suggested how you can shop to get the most nutrient-dense food for your money.

Carbohydrates: Grains, Breads, Pasta, Potatoes

The grains that have the most nutrients are whole grains – brown rice, oats, millet, quinoa, buckwheat, corn, whole wheat. These not only offer carbohydrates but vitamins, minerals, fiber, protein and healthful fats. Refined grains like white rice, white bread and pasta contribute to the metabolism of energy but you need to combine them with fruits, vegetables and a little protein and fat to supply the full array of nutrients. When shopping for breads look for loaves that have only a few simple ingredients. Wheat flour, yeast, water, salt and a small amount of sweetener are all you need to make a fine loaf of high-quality bread.

Some high-quality carbohydrates include:

corn tortillas	rice, brown
crackers	rice, white
kasha	soba noodles
linguini	spaghetti
macaroni	squash, winter
millet	sweet potatoes
oatmeal	udon noodles
polenta	whole grain bread
potatoes	whole grain pancakes
quinoa	whole wheat tortillas
rice cakes	

Vitamin & Mineral Rich Foods: Vegetables and Fruits

The mantra to use when shopping for produce is:
Fresh, Local, Organic, Seasonal.

Fresh produce not only has lots of needed vitamins and minerals but enzymes that help metabolize the nutrients. Frozen or canned foods are often missing enzymes and their nutrient value can be reduced in processing.

Fresh fruits and vegetables are alive. The longer the time from picking to your plate, the more nutrients that are lost. Local produce hasn't had far to travel.

National organic standards are detailed and comprehensive. If you buy a product labeled organic you can be sure that it has not been grown with pesticides, irradiated or genetically modified.

Seasonal food is at the peak of flavor and nutrient content. Eating foods that are in season and grown in your area can help your body adapt to the climate you live in.

Some high-quality vegetables and fruits include:

apples	lettuce
apricots	mango
bananas	melon
beets	onions
blueberries	oranges
broccoli	peppers
cabbage	pineapple
carrots	plums
cauliflower	raisins
celery	spinach
collard greens	sprouts
corn	strawberries
eggplant	tomatoes
grapefruit	zucchini
green beans	

Protein: Beans, Eggs, Fish, Chicken, Beef, Pork

In terms of ecological issues, long-term evidence suggests that it is worthwhile to seek out animal foods from animals that have been raised in a healthy way. That means eggs from chickens that have been allowed to move and peck freely, fish that have been caught in a river or an ocean as opposed to farm-raised, and chicken, beef, pork and dairy products from animals that have not been given antibiotics and hormones.

Some high-quality protein foods include:

baked beans	salmon
black beans	shrimp
chicken	sole
eggs	split peas
halibut	tempeh
kidney beans	tofu
lentils	tuna
pinto beans	

Fats: Olive Oil, Butter, Cheese, Nuts, Dressings

To avoid rancid fats, focus on fats that have been carefully handled and come from whole foods sources. Choose butter and cheeses that come from animals that have been allowed to graze on grass and not been given antibiotics and hormones. Buy raw nuts and seeds instead of those pre-roasted in cheap oils. Choose high-quality, stable oils to cook with such as extra-virgin olive oil and unrefined sesame oil. Know that most pale yellow, tasteless, odorless oils have been deodorized, filtered and refined, often using chemical solvents and high heat to extract the oil.

Some high-quality fats include:

almonds	olive oil
avocados	peanuts
butter	pecans
cashews	salad dressings
hazelnuts	sunflower seeds
nut butters	walnuts

New Players

Following are some ingredients that you may not be familiar with that are used in some of the recipes.

Arrowroot comes from a tropical plant whose tuberous root is dried and ground into a fine powder. It thickens liquid when heated. Cornstarch, a more highly processed thickener, can be substituted.

Basmati Brown Rice is a long slender whole grain with a distinctly aromatic flavor. Basmati rice is popular in Indian and Pakistani cultures. It can be stored in an airtight container on the shelf for 6-9 months.

Brown Rice Vinegar is a mild, delicate vinegar made from fermented brown rice. It is less acidic than most vinegars. You can substitute apple cider vinegar or other types of rice vinegar for brown rice vinegar.

Buckwheat Flour comes from finely ground buckwheat groats. Buckwheat is a whole grain native to China and Eastern Europe that is no relation at all to wheat. Buckwheat flour gives a distinct earthy flavor to baked goods.

Flax Seeds are a small, shiny, golden brown seeds that come from the flax plant. They are a rich source of omega-3 fatty acids, which have important properties for strengthening immunity. For proper digestion, grind into a paste or meal before mixing with other ingredients.

Ghee is clarified butter used in traditional Indian cooking. The milk proteins in the butter are removed and only the fat remains. Unlike butter, ghee can hold high heat without scorching.

Maple Syrup is made from the boiled sap of sugar maple trees. About 40 gallons of sap (from nine trees) make 1 gallon of syrup. Maple syrup is available in three grades: A, B or C, determined by the temperature used and length of time cooked. Read labels. Many syrups labeled "maple syrup" are actually a combination of corn syrups and flavorings. Use pure maple syrup. Honey can be substituted.

High Performance Recipes

Sweet Treats

Fundamentals

Psyched Up Smoothie

This recipe is for a single serving of smoothie. Orange or apple juice work well and our favorite frozen fruit to use is strawberries. Perfect pre-game or post-game snack.

½ ripe banana
½ cup frozen fruit
½ cup fruit juice
¼ cup yogurt
1 teaspoon sweetener (honey, maple syrup, sugar)

Place all ingredients in the blender and blend until smooth.

Prep time: 5 minutes
Makes a little over 1 cup

Sideline Lemonade

There's nothing fresher tasting than homemade lemonade. I bring a big thermos of this to hot weather games and the kids really appreciate it before the game and at halftime.

2 cups water
¾ cup fresh lemon juice
½ cup sugar or sucanat
2 teaspoons lemon zest, minced

Bring water to boil. Add lemon juice, sugar and zest. Simmer about 10 minutes, until sugar is dissolved. Put in a bottle or jar and let cool. Add enough cold fresh water to make 1 quart of lemonade. Serve over ice.

Prep time: 15 minutes
Makes 1 quart

Note: It is difficult to find pre-made lemonade that doesn't contain high fructose corn syrup or other chemical sweeteners. But Odwalla, Trader Joe's, and Nantucket Nectars make tasty lemonades that are simply sweetened with sugar. Dilute these and other 100% juice products for better hydration.

Dr. Murdoch's
Dangerous Date Shake

Brave, health-conscious players may dare to blend up this very nutrient-dense concoction for a pre-game boost. Soy milk or regular cow's milk can be substituted for rice milk. Flax seeds can be purchased whole and ground in a small coffee grinder. This assures that the nutritious oils found in the seeds stay fresh.

> **3 cups rice milk**
> **3-5 large dates, pits removed**
> **1 tablespoon almond or peanut butter**
> **¼ cup wheat germ**
> **2 tablespoons ground flax seeds (or flax meal)**

Freeze 1 cup of the rice milk in ice cube trays; this will take about 2 hours so you'll need to plan ahead. Soak dates in 1 cup of warm water until they soften. Drain water from dates and combine with all other ingredients in the blender. Blend until smooth. Add the rest of the rice milk to desired consistency.

Makes 2-4 servings
Prep time: 10 minutes

Outta Here Oat Waffles

*This unique waffle has no flour but uses highly digestible soaked whole grains. Adapted by Bastyr student Ronit Gourarie from **The Splendid Grain** cookbook by Rebecca Wood (William Morrow and Company, Inc., 1997) with a twirl from my friend Gay Stielstra. The batter will also make hearty and delicious pancakes.*

2 cups rolled oats
2½ - 2 ¾ cups milk (cow, soy, rice, nut, or buttermilk)
2 eggs
¼ teaspoon sea salt
2 tablespoons brown sugar or sucanat
1 teaspoon baking powder
½ teaspoon grated nutmeg
2-4 tablespoons melted butter

Combine oats and milk in blender. Cover and let soak, refrigerated, overnight for 8 hours. After soaking, add remaining ingredients and blend until smooth. Preheat an oiled or non-stick waffle iron. Pour about ½ cup of batter onto waffle iron, and cook for about 5 minutes or until golden. Repeat for remainder of batter. Serve hot with butter and warm maple syrup or applesauce.

Prep time: 15 minutes plus 8 hours soaking time
Makes 6 waffles

Grandslam Granola

Homemade granola makes an excellent pre-game breakfast or post-game snack. It travels well in a ziplock baggie. Any nuts and seeds that you like can be substituted for the ones listed.

3 cups rolled oats
½ cup sesame seeds
½ cup sunflower seeds
½ cup pumpkin seeds
½ cup almonds, chopped
½ cup whole wheat pastry flour
½ teaspoon cinnamon
Pinch sea salt
½ cup melted butter
½ cup maple syrup
1 teaspoon vanilla
¼ teaspoon almond extract

Optional Additions:

Raisins
Shredded coconut

Preheat oven to 300° F. In a large mixing bowl, combine oats, seeds, almonds, flour, cinnamon and salt; mix well. In a separate bowl, combine butter, syrup, and extracts. Slowly pour wet ingredients over dry ingredients, using a spatula to fold and evenly coat the dry mixture with the wet. Spread on cookie sheet or in a shallow pan and bake. Turn granola every 15 or 20 minutes so that it toasts evenly. Bake until granola is dry and golden (45-60 minutes). Add any optional ingredients after granola has cooled. Store in airtight jar.

Preparation time: 70 minutes
Makes 8 cups

Flipturn Flapjacks

A perfect pre-game breakfast — lots of carbohydrates plus a small amount of protein. The whole grain pancakes have staying power when there is a long travel time to the game.

> 1 egg
> 1½ cups dry whole-grain pancake mix (page 94)
> 1 cup buttermilk
> ½ cup water
> oil for griddle

Separate egg, pour egg white in one bowl and yolk in another. Beat egg white with an electric mixer until stiff peaks form. Set aside. In a large bowl, combine egg yolk, dry mix, buttermilk, and water. Mix thoroughly with a whisk. Gently fold egg white into batter.

Heat griddle to medium-high and coat surface with small amount of oil. Pour enough batter onto griddle to form a 5-inch diameter pancake. When pancake has cooked on the bottom, flip with a spatula and cook the other side. Keep cooked pancakes in a warm oven until ready to serve.

Preparation time: 25-30 minutes
Makes 10 five-inch pancakes

Sweet Spot Sweet Potato Soup

Sweet potatoes are loaded with all the right stuff – vitamin A, vitamin C, carbohydrates. Serve this creamy autumn orange soup with your favorite sandwich for a warm pre-game meal.

1 tablespoon butter
1 onion, chopped
1 teaspoon cumin
1 teaspoon coriander
pinch of cayenne
1 teaspoon salt
2 pounds sweet potatoes
4 cups chicken broth
2 tablespoons chopped parsley or cilantro

Heat butter in a 4-quart soup pot. Add onion and sauté until soft. Add spices and salt. Peel sweet potatoes and cut into chunks. Add sweet potatoes and broth to onions. Bring to boil. Lower heat, cover, and let simmer for about 30 minutes, until potatoes are fork tender. Blend soup in small batches in electric blender until smooth. Transfer blended soup to another pot or serving bowl. Garnish with parsley or cilantro and serve.

Preparation time: 40 minutes
Makes about 8 cups

110% Chicken Noodle Soup

Simple and delicious, this soup ranked second best in our team's pre-game meal survey. I use the chicken breast from making the stock (page 90) to complete the soup. Any size noodle works but my favorite is organic ribbons. You'll notice I've also used bok choy to increase the nutritional benefits. Any dark green vegetable can be substituted or you can omit this ingredient altogether.

1 tablespoon butter
1 onion, chopped
1 clove garlic, minced
1 carrot, sliced
1 stalk celery, diced
5 leaves bok choy (optional)
1½ quarts chicken stock (page 90)
1½ cups cooked chicken, cut into bite-size pieces
2 cups cooked noodles
2 tablespoons chopped fresh rosemary
2 tablespoons chopped fresh marjoram
2 tablespoons chopped fresh parsley
salt and pepper to taste

Heat butter in a soup pot. Add onion and garlic and sauté until soft. Add carrot and celery and continue sautéing. Cut white part of bok choy leaves into ½-inch pieces. Roll dark green part of leaves and slice into thin strips and set aside. Add white part of bok choy to onion-carrot-celery mixture.

Add stock, chicken, and noodles and raise the heat until soup comes to a boil. Turn the heat off or remove pot from stove, add fresh herbs and strips of bok choy, cover, and let sit 15 minutes. Taste soup and add salt and freshly ground pepper to bring up the flavor.

Preparation time: 30 minutes
Makes 6 big bowls of soup

Full Press Potato Soup

A simple carbohydrate-laden soup with added protein from the stock and yogurt. You can peel the potatoes or not. Peeled potatoes produce a creamier texture, but there is extra nutritive value in the peels if you don't mind a coarser soup. Serve with a salad and/or sandwich two hours before practice or game.

1 tablespoon butter
1 onion, chopped
1 large clove garlic, minced
1 stalk celery, chopped
3-4 cups potato chunks
2 cups chicken stock (page 90)
¼ cup plain whole milk yogurt
sea salt
freshly ground black pepper
¼ cup fresh chives or parsley

Heat butter in a soup pot. Add onion, garlic, and celery and sauté until onion is soft. Add potatoes and stock. Bring to simmer and cook until potatoes are tender, about 15 minutes. Remove from heat and let cool slightly. Put soup and yogurt in blender and blend until smooth. Add salt and pepper to taste. Garnish with chives or parsley.

Prep time: 30 minutes
Makes 4 servings

Big Mo Minestrone

Minestrone means "big soup" in Italian and there are as many variations as there are cooks. I've used some of the classic minestrone vegetables, but my friend Elena says don't hesitate to add any vegetable your heart desires. Serve this with lots of freshly grated Parmesan and good hearty bread to build momentum for that next practice or game.

½ cup extra-virgin olive oil
1 tablespoon butter
2 cloves garlic, minced
1 large onion, diced
2 medium carrots, sliced
2 stalks celery, diced
1 medium potato, diced
1 15-ounce can diced tomatoes
1 teaspoon dried oregano
2 teaspoons salt
4 cups chicken broth
1 cup fresh or frozen corn
1 cup green beans, cut into 1½" pieces
1 15-ounce can kidney beans, drained and rinsed
black pepper
½ cup chopped fresh basil (optional)
Parmesan cheese

In a large soup pot over medium heat add olive oil, butter, garlic and onion. Sauté until onion is soft. Add carrots, celery, potato and sauté about 5 minutes more. Add tomatoes, oregano, salt and chicken broth. Bring heat up to simmer. Cover and cook ½ hour. Add corn, green beans and kidney beans and simmer for another 5 minutes or until green beans are tender. Stir in fresh basil and black pepper to taste. Serve with freshly grated Parmesan on top.

Preparation time: 45 minutes
Makes 6-8 servings

Skill-Building Greens with Lime Vinaigrette

If you're a player who enjoys salad this is a nice combination of greens with a slightly tart dressing. I find it goes well with enchiladas, black beans and other Southwestern dishes. The toasted pumpkin seeds and avocado add excellent fats and more caloric value to the salad.

Salad:

¼ cup toasted pumpkin seeds
¼ head of leaf lettuce
¼ bunch spinach
¼ bunch arugula or rocket
1 scallion, finely sliced
½ ripe avocado, sliced

Dressing:

2 teaspoons rice vinegar
Juice of 1 lime
⅛ teaspoon ground cumin
⅛ teaspoon ground cardamom
1 small clove garlic, minced
¼ teaspoon sea salt
3 tablespoons extra-virgin olive oil

Put pumpkin seeds in a skillet warmed to medium heat. Move skillet and constantly stir seeds until they begin to pop, puff up and give off a nice aroma. Remove from skillet and set aside.

Wash lettuce and greens by placing leaves in a sink full of cold water. Drain and repeat. Spin or pat dry. Tear greens into bite-sized pieces and place in a large salad bowl. Add all other salad ingredients except avocado. Put all ingredients for dressing except oil in a small bowl. Whisk in the olive oil. Taste and adjust for salt and tartness. Peel and slice avocado. Add avocado, toasted pumpkin seeds and dressing just before serving and toss well.

Preparation time: 20 minutes
Makes 4 servings

Pacesetter Salad
with Orange Vinaigrette

Karen Conger, a student from the university where I teach, invented this salad. The addition of cheese, grapes, walnuts and cranberries make it quite hearty. A great accompaniment to soup and bread.

Dressing:

1 teaspoon orange zest
¼ cup orange juice
2 teaspoons balsamic vinegar
3 tablespoons olive oil
salt and pepper to taste

Salad:

⅓ cup toasted walnuts
2 cups red leaf lettuce
1 cup arugula
2 cups baby spinach
¼ cup bleu cheese, crumbled
½ cup red grapes, halved
⅓ cup dried cranberries

Combine all dressing ingredients in a bowl and whisk together. Set aside. Preheat oven to 300° F. Put walnuts in baking dish and toast in oven for 12-15 minutes, until they give off aroma. Remove nuts from oven and cool. Fill sink with cold water, add all greens, removing any tough stems. Drain, and repeat. Spin dry. Tear into bite-size pieces and place in salad bowl. Add toasted walnuts, cheese, grapes, and cranberries to greens. Add dressing to salad, toss, and serve immediately.

Preparation time: 20 minutes
Makes 4-6 servings

All Net Spinach Salad

Serve with warm garlic bread or foccacia for a light pre-game meal.
Add a sliced hard-boiled egg for extra protein if desired.

Salad:

⅓ cup glazed pecans (see "Goalkick Glazed Nuts"
    recipe, page 60)
1 bunch spinach
½ small red onion, sliced in thin rounds
¼ cup crumbled feta cheese

Dressing:

3 tablespoons extra-virgin olive oil
2 tablespoons balsamic vinegar
1 teaspoon maple syrup
¾ teaspoon Dijon mustard
¼ teaspoon fresh ground pepper

Prepare glazed nuts. Remove stems from spinach. Wash by
placing leaves in a sink full of cold water. Drain and repeat.
Spin or pat dry. Tear spinach into bite-sized pieces. Place in a
large salad bowl. Add cooled nuts, red onion and cheese to
spinach. Place all dressing ingredients in a small bowl and whisk
together. Dress salad just before serving.

Preparation: 10 minutes
Makes 6 servings

Goalkick Glazed Nuts

This are delicious on hot cereal, in a fresh green salad or tossed in a pasta or rice dish. They also work nicely as a quick post-game snack.

Extra-virgin olive oil or butter
⅓ cup pecans or walnuts
1 tablespoon maple syrup
pinch of sea salt
one grind of black pepper
tiny pinch of cayenne

Preheat oven to 325° F. Lightly coat baking pan with olive oil or butter. Combine pecans, syrup, salt, pepper, and cayenne in a small bowl and toss to coat. Spread nut mixture into baking dish. Bake until nuts are golden and glazed, but not wet – about 15 minutes. Stir occasionally to break up clumps. Cool completely on baking sheet.

Makes ⅓ cup
Prep time: 20 minutes

Freestyle Sweet Potatoes

The vegetables with the most vitamins and minerals are the dark green ones and the yellow and orange vegetables. Sweet potatoes needn't be saved for Thanksgiving dinner. They are an easy-to-prepare, nutritious pre-game food.

> 2-3 sweet potatoes, scrubbed and cut in chunks
> 3 tablespoons extra-virgin olive oil
> 2 teaspoons cumin
> ¼ teaspoon cayenne
> ⅛ teaspoon cinnamon

Preheat oven to 350° F. Cut sweet potatoes and place in an 8x8" baking dish. Mix oil and spices together in a small bowl and drizzle over top of the vegetables. Mix vegetables with a wooden spoon so they are evenly coated. Cover pan and bake 45 minutes.

Preparation time: 1 hour
Makes 4 servings

Give and Go Garlic Greens

The most nutrient-dense, vitamin-rich, energizing vegetables on the planet are dark leafy greens. They're easy to make and help give players radiant complexions.

1 large bunch of collards, kale, bok choy, or Swiss chard
1 tablespoon extra virgin olive oil
1 tablespoon minced garlic

Garnish:
½ -1 teaspoon brown rice vinegar
½ teaspoon tamari

For greens with tough stems, cut the leaves away from the stem before washing. Wash greens carefully. An easy way is to fill your sink with cold water and submerge the greens. If the water has a lot of sediment, drain the sink and repeat. Stack leaves on top of one another and chop into thin strips.

Heat oil in a 10-inch skillet. Add garlic and sauté a minute or so. Add greens and keep them moving in the skillet. Turn frequently so that all greens reach the heat. When all greens have turned bright green and begun to wilt, taste a strip. When you chew it, the juice should be sweet, not bitter. If it is bitter, cook the greens a bit longer. When the greens are tender and sweet, remove from heat. Sprinkle vinegar and tamari over the top. Toss gently and serve.

Preparation time: 15 minutes
Makes 2 cups, 4 servings

Last Lap Potato Salad

This potato salad will travel much better than those made with mayonnaise. Should stay fine in the cooler for several hours. Any type of cooked potato dish (except french fries) will give the athlete good pre-game carbohydrate fuel. For an even simpler version of this dish, cook the potatoes and dress while warm with Pesto Sauce (page 95).

Salad:

6-8 cups cubed red potatoes

Dressing:

3-4 cloves garlic
½ cup tightly packed fresh basil
½ teaspoon sea salt
1 teaspoon lemon zest
3-4 tablespoons extra-virgin olive oil
3-4 tablespoons freshly squeezed lemon juice

Wash, scrub, and cut potatoes in large chunks. Place potatoes in large pot of boiling water. Cook 10-12 minutes or until just tender. While potatoes are cooking, place garlic, basil, salt, and lemon zest on cutting board. Chop together to a paste-like consistency. Combine paste with oil and lemon juice; set aside. Drain potatoes and let cool. Pour dressing over slightly warm potatoes; toss gently. Serve immediately or chill to serve later.

Preparation time: 20 minutes
Makes 6 servings

Slam Dunk Sesame Noodles

Compliments to the lovely creator of this recipe, My-Duyen Huynh. These noodles are exceedingly popular with children of all ages. You can be quite creative with your choice of vegetables. We have written it using cabbage, carrots, and celery, but broccoli, bok choy, or red pepper are just a few alternate choices. Makes a top-notch pre-game meal.

¼ cup sesame seeds
8 ounces angel hair noodles
5 stalks celery, cut at an angle into thin strips
2 large carrots, cut in thin strips
½ head of cabbage, cut into thin strips
6 cloves garlic, minced
about ½ cup olive oil
1 teaspoon sugar
1 teaspoon sea salt
½ cup chopped cilantro and green onion
1 teaspoon toasted sesame oil
¼ cup soy sauce (or to taste)
black pepper

In a large skillet or wok, toast sesame seeds over medium heat, stirring constantly, until they turn golden and give off aroma. Remove from pan and set aside. Cook noodles according to package directions. Drain and place in a large bowl.

Get all vegetables and garlic cut and ready to go. Heat about 4 tablespoons of oil in skillet or wok. Add ½ of the garlic, ½ of the celery and carrots, ½ teaspoon of sugar and salt. Cook, stirring constantly until vegetables are bright and crisp. Remove from pan and add to noodles. Repeat this process of sautéing with the other half of the vegetables.

Toss cooked vegetables with noodles – you will probably need to use your hands. Add cilantro and green onion, sesame oil, soy sauce, black pepper, and toasted sesame seeds. Toss again until even. Taste. Add more soy sauce if desired.

Preparation time: 30 minutes
Makes 8 servings

Fast Break
Garlic Mashed Potatoes

Most of you probably have your own method of making mashed potatoes, but you can save time and intensify flavor by using a pressure cooker to make mashers. Use small yellow Finn or red potatoes and leave the skins on to increase the nutrient value.

6-8 yellow Finn or red potatoes (about 2 pounds)
1 cup water
½ teaspoon sea salt
5 cloves garlic, peeled and left whole
2 tablespoons milk or half & half
1-2 tablespoons butter
salt and pepper to taste

Wash and scrub potatoes and cut each in half, quarter if large. Put potatoes, water, salt, and garlic in pressure cooker and secure lid. Bring heat up until pressure comes up. Lower heat slightly and pressure cook for 10 minutes. Allow pressure to come down or run cool water over top of pot until pressure comes down. Add milk, butter, and salt and pepper to hot potatoes and whip with an electric mixer until smooth.

Preparation time: 15-20 minutes
Makes 4 servings

Turn Up the Heat BBQ Beans

This recipe is gleaned from Mary Shaw's "Main Course." The BBQ sauce is excellent and can be used in many creative ways. Serve these beans with mashed potatoes or cornbread and coleslaw for a high carbohydrate pre- or post-game meal.

1 cup pinto beans, soaked overnight

1 tablespoon olive oil
½ onion, chopped
3 cloves garlic, minced
4 ounces canned tomato paste
¼ cup apple cider vinegar
¼ cup maple syrup
4 teaspoons molasses
1 teaspoon Dijon mustard
pinch of chipotle chili powder or cayenne
½ cup bean cooking liquid or water
1 teaspoon sea salt

Drain off soaking water and place soaked beans in a large pot. Add 3 cups of fresh water and bring beans to a boil. Lower heat and simmer until tender, about an hour. A quicker cooking method is pressure cooking (see page 93). You may also use canned beans (2-3 cups) to save time.

Drain beans reserving cooking liquid and set aside. Heat oil in a large skillet. Sauté onion and garlic until soft. Add drained beans. Whisk together tomato paste, vinegar, syrup, molasses, mustard, chili powder and liquid in a bowl. Add the tomato sauce to beans and simmer about 10 minutes until it thickens.

Preparation time: 1 hour
Makes 4-6 servings

Unsurpassed Polenta with Asiago

Polenta is coarsely ground corn meal that is cooked and served as a kind of mush or cooked, allowed to set and then sliced. Getting the mouthwatering creamy texture requires long, slow stirring. It helps build a player's concentration and stamina to do this task.

2 cups vegetable or chicken stock
3 cups water
½ teaspoon salt
1 tablespoon extra-virgin olive oil or butter
1 cup polenta or corn grits
4-6 tablespoons Asiago or Parmesan cheese
olive oil

Bring stock and water to boil. Add salt and oil or butter. Slowly add polenta, stirring continuously with a whisk. Lower heat to where the mixture puckers, but doesn't spit. Continue stirring in a clockwise motion with a wooden spoon for 30-40 minutes until smooth and thick (individual grains can't be seen). Stir in grated cheese. Lightly oil a pie plate. Pour polenta into pie plate and smooth the top. Let cool completely.

To reheat, remove from pan. Preheat broiler. Brush top of polenta with olive oil and broil 3 minutes. Remove, slice and serve.

Preparation time: 50 minutes plus cooling time
Makes 8 slices

Clear the Bar Hoppin' John

Great served with polenta or corn bread and greens. A good luck, high carbohydrate, hip-hoppin' meal.

1 tablespoon olive oil or butter
1 onion, chopped
5-6 cloves of garlic, minced
½ red bell pepper, diced
1 carrot, sliced in rounds
½ cup corn kernels
½ cup chopped tomatoes
1 tablespoon fresh thyme
½ teaspoon salt
⅛ teaspoon black pepper
¼-½ teaspoon red pepper flakes
2-3 cups cooked black-eyed peas (page 94)
2 scallions, chopped

Heat oil or butter in skillet. Add onion and garlic and sauté until onion is soft and translucent. Add red pepper and carrot and sauté a few minutes more. Add corn, chopped tomatoes, thyme, salt, pepper and red pepper flakes (add larger amount for more hop to the john). Stir gently until heated through.

Stir in cooked peas. Taste and adjust seasonings. Add scallions just prior to serving.

Makes 4-6 servings
Prep time: 30 minutes

Corner Kick Cornbread

From the talented Jeff Basom, chef at Bastyr University. Serve with hot soup before games or carry a slice in your bag to take advantage of the post-game glycogen window (see page 25).

1 cup unbleached white flour
1 cup fine cornmeal
1½ teaspoons baking powder
½ teaspoon baking soda
½ teaspoon sea salt
2 eggs
¼ cup honey
⅔ cup buttermilk
4 tablespoons butter, melted

Preheat oven to 350° F. Mix dry ingredients in a 4-quart bowl. Set aside. In a small bowl, beat eggs. Add honey and mix well. Add buttermilk and melted butter to eggs and honey. Mix well and add all at once to dry ingredients folding wet into dry, mixing just enough to moisten all of the flour. Lightly grease a loaf pan and pour batter in. Bake until golden brown and springy to the touch – about 30-40 minutes.

Prep time: 45-50 minutes
Makes one loaf (8 thick slices)

Man-to-Man Black Bean Stew

Serve this yummy stew over white or brown rice or with warm tortillas for a delicious, carbohydrate-rich meal. Mexican seasoning blends come in bulk or spice bottles at the grocery store. They are usually a combination of cumin, oregano, peppers and other spices that offer a Southwestern flavor to dishes.

1 teaspoon extra-virgin olive oil
1 onion, chopped
2 cloves garlic, minced
1 teaspoon ground cumin
2 teaspoons Mexican seasoning
1 cup dried black beans, soaked
1 dried chipotle chili
2 cups soup stock or water
1-2 teaspoons sea salt
½ cup frozen corn kernels
½ cup chopped tomatoes
⅓ cup chopped cilantro
lime
sour cream

Heat oil in a large pot. Add onion, garlic, cumin, and Mexican seasoning and sauté until onions are soft. Drain soaking water off beans. Add soaked beans, chipotle chili and stock or water to onions and spices. Raise heat and bring to boil. Lower heat, and simmer 1 hour + until beans are tender. (Pressure cooking beans is also an option, see recipe page 93.) Salt to taste. Add corn, tomatoes, and cilantro. Serve garnished with a squeeze of lime and sour cream dollop.

Preparation time: 1½ - 2 hours
Makes about 4 cups of soup

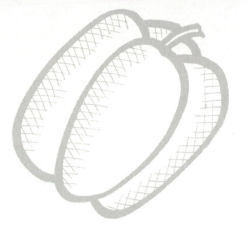

Grace's One Touch Quesadillas

Created by #7 on the FCA Momentum. Serve with salad and Man-to-Man Black Bean Stew (page 70) for a jump start pre-game meal.

Additional Filling Ideas:
    finely diced jalapenos
    chopped cilantro
    chopped fresh tomatoes
    chopped scallion
    sautéed onions and green peppers
    roasted red pepper
    grilled chicken strips

    2 cups grated cheese (cheddar, jack, or mozarella)
    4 teaspoons butter
    4 flour tortillas
    1 cup filling (any combination of ingredients listed)
    salsa

Prepare 1 cup of the additional filling ingredients you plan to use and combine together with grated cheese in a bowl. Heat a large skillet on low to medium heat. Add 1 teaspoon of butter. Lay 1 tortilla in the skillet and warm it until it is flexible. Place ¾ cup of the filling on one half of the tortilla. Fold in half and press down slightly with a spatula. Cover the skillet with a lid and let quesadilla heat for 1 minute. Remove cover, flip quesadilla over, press down with spatula, cover skillet and heat one more minute. Repeat process with the other 3 tortillas. Cut each of the 4 quesadillas in half to make 8. Serve with salsa or other dipping sauce.

Preparation time: 10-15 minutes
Makes 8 servings

Final Buzzer Fried Rice

Brown rice is an excellent carbohydrate to use to fuel up athletes of all ages. You can transform ordinary brown rice into a more appealing and nutritious dish by adding sautéed spices and vegetables. White rice can be substituted.

3 tablespoons butter, ghee, or olive oil
1-2 teaspoons ground cumin
1-2 teaspoons ground coriander
pinch of cayenne (optional)
¼ cup pine nuts or split cashews
3 scallions
¼ cup dried currants
⅓ cup frozen peas
2-3 cups cooked basmati brown rice (page 91)

Heat butter in a large skillet over low to medium heat. Add spices and nuts and allow them produce a fragrance, the nuts changing to a golden color. Add scallions and sauté until bright green. Add currants and peas and sauté a minute or two more. Slowly add rice, breaking it up so it gets evenly coated. When all the rice has been added, keep stirring until the dish is mixed well and evenly heated.

Preparation time: 15 minutes
Makes 4-6 servings

Fast Flexible Fettucine

Here's quick, easy, nutritious food for growing athletes. The best Parmesan to use, according to recipe author Elena Leonard, is parmiggiano regianno imported from Italy which is now available in many grocery stores. Romano peccorino (sheep cheese) is also nice.

> 1 pound dry pasta
> 2 tablespoons salt
> 3 eggs
> ⅓ cup chopped Italian parsley
> freshly grated Parmesan

Cook the pasta in 4 quarts of water with the salt until just tender. Beat the eggs. Drain the pasta quickly and put it back in the pot. Pour in the beaten eggs and stir. The heat of the just-cooked pasta will cook the egg onto it. Stir in the parsley. Serve with plenty of freshly grated parmesan.

Preparation time: 15-20 minutes
Makes 6-8 servings

Game Face Fish Tacos

These are just like the yummy ones you can get at restaurants only better – the fish isn't deep-fried and the ingredients are fresh! You can choose to use soft corn tortillas or crisp taco shells. Two or three limes should give you all the juice you need for this recipe. Make plenty, they're good.

> 1 tablespoon lime juice
> 1 tablespoon extra-virgin olive oil
> 1 tablespoon tamari or soy sauce
> 1 lb. fish, true cod, halibut or other white fish
> 8-12 corn tortillas or taco shells
> grated cheese
> salsa

Sauce:
> ¼ cup mayonaise
> 1 tablespoon lime juice
> 2 tablespoons chopped cilantro
> 1 clove garlic, pressed
> ⅛ teaspoon cumin
> 1 tablespoon water

Vegetables:
> ½ cup shredded cabbage
> 4 leaves romaine, rolled and cut in thin strips
> 1 carrot, grated
> ¼ cup chopped red onion
> 1 tablespoon extra-virgin olive oil
> 1 tablespoon lime juice
> salt and pepper

Combine 1 tablespoon each of lime juice, olive oil and soy sauce in a small bowl and pour over fish. Allow fish to marinate for at least ½ hour.

Combine all ingredients for sauce in a small bowl and whisk until smooth. Cut, grate, and chop vegetables. Dress with olive oil, lime juice, salt and pepper and toss. Set aside dressed vegetables and sauce.

Preheat broiler. Place marinated fish on a broiler pan and broil about 10-15 minutes depending on the thickness of the fish (10 minutes per inch). Warm tortillas in a skillet one at a time or bake taco shells. When fish is done, cut into small slices. Place a few fish slices in tortilla with dressed vegetables on top. Pour a tablespoon or two of the sauce over the top and add a bit of grated cheese and salsa if desired. Repeat process for each tortilla. Serve immediately.

Preparation time: 45 minutes
Makes ⅔ cup sauce, 8-12 tacos

Crack of the Bat
Vegetable Curry

Serve this super-nutritious, super-tasty curry dish over rice with a green salad on the side and raita (yogurt topping) and you have a pre-game meal fit for a king.

2 teaspoons extra-virgin olive oil or ghee
1 onion, chopped
1 clove garlic, minced
½ teaspoon sea salt
2 teaspoons ground coriander
2 teaspoons ground cumin
1 teaspoon turmeric
½ teaspoon cinnamon
pinch of cayenne
3 small potatoes, cut in chunks
1 carrot, sliced
1 cup tomato sauce
½ cup water
1 cup cooked chickpeas (page 93)

Garnish:
Classic Raita (page 77)

Heat oil in a large pot. Add onion, garlic, and salt; sauté until onion is soft. Add coriander, cumin, turmeric, cinnamon, and cayenne. Add potatoes, carrots, tomato sauce, and water; stir well. Bring to boil, lower heat and simmer, covered, until potatoes and carrots are tender, about 20 minutes. Add cooked chickpeas and stir in gently. Serve over rice and garnish with raita on top.

Preparation time: 30-35 minutes
Makes 4 servings

Classic Raita

> 1 cup plain organic whole milk yogurt
> ½ cucumber, peeled, seeded, and diced
> 1 scallion, finely chopped
> 1 teaspoon finely chopped mint
> ½ teaspoon cumin, ground
> pinch of cayenne
> salt and pepper to taste

Combine all ingredients together in a small bowl. Serve immediately or chill for 30 minutes.

For an even thicker and creamier topping, start with 2 cups of yogurt. Line a colander or strainer with cheesecloth. Pour yogurt in the cheesecloth, set colander or strainer over a bowl, and strain overnight in the refrigerator. This will produce about 1 cup of yogurt cream. Add the rest of the ingredients to the yogurt cream. Let set and serve.

Preparation time: Depends on how you make it.
Makes 1½ cups

Time Out for Chicken Teriyaki

Make mounds of rice and serve this easy-to-make, kid-pleasing dish heaped on top. Perfect blend of carbohydrates, vitamin-rich vegetables and protein to fuel-up the athletic body. Use any combination of vegetables.

⅓ cup ~~extra-virgin olive oil~~ *soy sauce*
1 teaspoon grated ginger root
3-4 tablespoons honey
1 tablespoon brown sugar
1 small clove garlic, minced
½ cup water
1 pound chicken breasts, boneless, skinless
½ head green cabbage, shredded
1 carrot, cut at a diagonal in slices
½ medium onion, cut in chunks
2-3 tablespoons high-oleic safflower or peanut oil
2 teaspoons arrowroot

Blend together all ingredients for teriyaki sauce together in a saucepan and warm on low until sugar dissolves. Remove from heat. Prepare chicken breasts. Pound out until even in thickness and cut into small strips. Put in a bowl or dish and cover with ¼ - ⅓ cup of the teriyaki sauce. (The chicken can marinate refrigerated for up to 8 hours. The longer it marinates, the deeper the flavors.)

Cut all vegetables. Heat ½ of oil in a wok or skillet. Stir fry vegetables until bright and crisp. Remove vegetables and set aside. Heat remaining oil in wok. Add chicken and stir fry until tender. Add arrowroot to sauce and stir it well, then pour remainder of sauce over chicken. Add cooked vegetables and toss until sauce thickens. Turn heat off, serve immediately over rice.

Preparation time: ½ hour
Makes 4 servings

Power Up Pesto Pasta and Smoked Salmon

This is quick and easy. Serve with a salad and you have a perfectly balanced pre-game plate. Baby broccoli is lovely in this dish but any green vegetable or a medley of vegetables will work fine – like green beans, snap peas, zucchini, bok choy. Go go go!

8-10 ounces pasta (ribbons, spirals, or penne are nice)
1 teaspoon salt
2 cups (or 1 bunch) baby broccoli or broccoli flowerettes
1 tablespoon butter
¼ lemon
salt and pepper
extra-virgin olive oil
½ cup pesto sauce (see page 95)
½ pound piece of smoked salmon

Heat a large pot of water to boiling. Add 1 teaspoon salt to boiling water, add pasta and cook according to package directions.

While pasta is cooking, cut broccoli into bite-size pieces or flowerettes. Heat butter in a large skillet to medium heat, below browning point. Add broccoli, and keep the vegetables moving in the skillet for 5-8 minutes until bright green and tender (taste a piece to tell – it should be juicy and sweet). Squeeze lemon over broccoli, season with salt and pepper and toss again.

Drain pasta well and return to pot. Drizzle with a little olive oil. Add pesto and toss gently until noodles are well-coated. Cut salmon into small pieces. Add salmon and broccoli to pasta, toss again and serve.

Preparation time: 20-25 minutes
Makes 3-4 servings

Victorious Vegetable Sushi Rolls

*Two-time Olympic gold medalist Michelle Smith lists sushi as one of her typical pre-competition meals. Carbohydrates from the rice and loads of vitamins and minerals from the nori and vegetables provide excellent fuel. Nori is available at natural foods stores and Asian markets. Thanks to Rebecca Wood's book, **The Splendid Grain**, for giving me new tips on Nori-Maki.*

4+ cups cooked rice (see pages 91 and 92)
¼ cup brown rice vinegar
2 tablespoons succanat or white sugar
½ teaspoon sea salt
4 sheets toasted nori

Filling:
slices of ripe avocado
cucumber strips

Dipping sauce:
3 tablespoons tamari
2 teaspoons grated gingeroot
1 tablespoon water
1 teaspoon wasabi powder mixed with 1 teaspoon water (optional)

After rice has cooked, let stand for 10 minutes. Combine vinegar, succanat and salt in a small sauce pan over low heat. Warm slightly to dissolve sugar and salt. Remove from heat. Spread rice out in a large bowl or pan. Sprinkle the vinegar solution over the rice as you gently toss it with a wooden spoon. Peel and slice avocado into strips. Peel and seed cucumber and cut into long strips.

Lay nori shiny side down on a bamboo mat. Spread 1-1½ cups of the rice mixture onto the nori leaving 1" uncovered at the top edge. Place strips of filling lengthwise in the middle of the rice. Lift bamboo rolling mat from edge nearest you and begin to roll, tucking firmly into the center while bending the mat up, taking care not to catch it in the roll. Gently squeeze the roll to make it even. Set the roll aside and repeat the procedure with the remaining nori. If not serving immediately, seal rolls with plastic wrap.

Using a wet, sharp knife, cut the rolls into equal pieces. Put all ingredients for dipping sauce together in a small attractive bowl. Serve sushi rolls with dipping sauce on the side.

Preparation time: 30 minutes, if rice pre-cooked
Makes 24 pieces

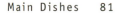

Overtime Quinoa and Black Bean Salad

You might not have heard of quinoa (pronounced keen-wah) but you should make its acquaintance. It's a very nutrient-dense, quick-cooking whole grain that has a light nutty flavor. Directions for how to prepare basic quinoa are on page 91.

¼ cup pine nuts
2½-3 cups cooked quinoa
¼ cup olive oil
¼ cup lemon juice
½ teaspoon ground cumin
½ teaspoon sea salt
5 tablespoons chopped cilantro
2 scallions, finely chopped
½ jalapeno pepper, finely chopped (seeds removed)
1 cup cooked black beans (page 93)

Pre-heat oven to 300° F. Put pine nuts in a small baking dish and toast them for 5-7 minutes, until they turn golden. Remove and set aside.

Remove cooked quinoa from pot, place in large bowl and let cool. Combine olive oil, lemon juice, cumin, and salt in a bowl. Whisk together and pour over warm quinoa (not hot, not cold). Toss well. Add cilantro, scallions, jalapeno, black beans, and toasted pine nuts to quinoa and toss again. Serve at room temperature.

Preparation time: 45-50 minutes
Serves 4

Give Your Best
Lemon Yogurt Treat

One of my students, Sandi Navarro, made up a variation of this for her final project. The lemon sauce is unique and adds a lot of sweet flavor and zip to simple yogurt and fruit. A heavenly breakfast with a little granola (page 51) thrown in or a zippy, easy-to-digest pre-game snack. Crystallized ginger can be found in Asian markets, Trader Joe's, and other specialty food stores.

Zest 1 lemon, chopped fine
¼ cup apple juice
¼ cup crystallized ginger, grated
Juice of 1 lemon
1 quart whole milk plain yogurt (see Brand Names page 30)
1 pint fresh blueberries, raspberries, or strawberries

Mix zest, apple juice and grated crystallized ginger in a small saucepan. Simmer about 5-10 minutes until ginger melts. Remove from heat and add lemon juice. Blend in blender. Set aside to cool.

Put yogurt in a bowl. Fold in the fruit. Place in individual serving bowls and top each serving with about 2 tablespoons of lemon sauce.

Preparation time: 10-15 minutes
Makes 8 small servings, 4 athlete-size servings

Breakaway Banana Date Bread

This moist, sweet bread uses various fruits for natural sweetness. To get extra sweetness from bananas, peel overripe ones and freeze them. Thaw before using. Great post-practice snack to pack in the sports bag.

1 cup whole wheat pastry flour
1 cup unbleached white flour
2 teaspoons non-aluminum baking powder
1 teaspoon baking soda
½ teaspoon sea salt

2 ripe bananas
⅓ cup melted, unsalted butter
10-12 pitted dates, chopped in pieces
½ cup orange juice
½ cup maple syrup
1 teaspoon vanilla
1 egg
⅓ cup chopped walnuts
½ cup raisins or currants

Preheat oven to 375° F. Mix flours, baking powder, soda, and salt together in a bowl, set aside. Put bananas, butter, dates, juice, maple syrup, and vanilla in the blender and blend until smooth. Add egg and pulse briefly. Add wet ingredients to dry mixture and mix well. Fold in chopped nuts and raisins. Put mixture in a lightly oiled 8x8 baking dish and bake for 35-40 minutes or until a knife inserted in the center comes out clean.

Preparation time: 1 hour
Makes 8-16 slices, depending on size of cuts

Rebound
Raspberry-Pecan Oat Bars

*Inspired by a recipe from Mary Estella's **Natural Foods Cookbook**. This makes a great post-game snack.*

2 cups rolled oats
1 cup whole wheat pastry flour
⅓ cup pecans, chopped
¼ teaspoon sea salt
6 tablespoons melted butter
6 tablespoons maple syrup
1 teaspoon vanilla
1 cup or 1 10-ounce jar raspberry jam

Preheat oven to 350° F. Combine oats, flour, pecans and salt in a mixing bowl. Add butter, maple syrup, and vanilla and mix well. Add a teaspoon or two of water if necessary to keep mixture moist.

Lightly oil an 8x8 baking dish. Take ½ of the oat mixture and press into the bottom with moist hands. Spread the jam on top. Crumble the remaining oat mix on top and press gently. Bake for 20 minutes. Let cool slightly before cutting into bars.

Preparation time: 30 minutes
Makes 8 large bars

Dig Deep Coconut Date Treats

These are very quick and easy to make. They're also easy to pack to go on the road and contain a wealth of readily absorbable calories. Yum yum, roll some up!

> ¾ cup roasted pecans, chopped
> ½ cup pitted dates, chopped
> ½ teaspoon orange zest
> ¼ teaspoon cinnamon
> pinch of salt
> 1 tablespoon maple syrup
> ¼ cup shredded coconut

Put all ingredients except coconut in food processor. Pulse until you have an even mealy texture. With moist hands, roll the mixture into 1-inch balls. Spread the coconut on a plate and roll each ball in the coconut, covering each one evenly.

Preparation time: 10 minutes
Makes 8-10 bonbons

Over the Hurdle Oatmeal Cookies

According to Mary Lou Basom's son, Jeff, these are the best oatmeal cookies in the world. Make a bunch for the team and hand them out after the game.

1 cup butter (room temperature)
1 cup brown sugar or sucanat
1 cup white sugar
1 teaspoon vanilla
2 eggs
1⅓ cups unbleached white flour
3 cups rolled oats
½ teaspoon salt
1 teaspoon baking soda
½ cup walnuts, chopped
¾ cup raisins

Preheat oven to 350° F. In a large mixing bowl, cream together butter, sugars, and vanilla. If using sucanat, run it through the blender or a small grinder first. It will incorporate better that way. Lightly beat eggs and add.

In a separate bowl combine flour, oats, salt, and soda. Add to wet ingredients and mix well. Fold in nuts and raisins. Roll into 1-inch balls and place on a cookie sheet. Bake 12-15 minutes.

Makes 3 dozen cookies
Prep time: 25-30 minutes

Final Stretch Chocolate Chip Cookies

Okay, if you're going to have a sweet treat at least go for something homemade from natural ingredients rather than indulge in pre-packaged baked goods made with cheap oils and high fructose corn syrup, right? I recommend Sunspire Organic Chocolate Chips, they're quite yummy.

1¼ cups whole wheat pastry flour
1¼ cups unbleached white flour
1½ teaspoons baking soda
1½ teaspoons baking powder
1 teaspoon sea salt
¾ cup soft unsalted butter
½ cup white sugar
¾ cup sucanat or brown sugar
2 eggs
1 teaspoon vanilla
1 cup chocolate chips
⅔ cup chopped nuts

Preheat oven to 350° F. Combine flours, baking soda, baking powder, and salt; set aside. In a separate bowl, cream together butter and sugars. If using sucanat, run it through the blender or a small grinder first. It will incorporate better that way. Beat in eggs and vanilla. Add flour mixture slowly. Stir in chocolate chips and nuts. Drop in heaping teaspoonfuls onto ungreased cookie sheet. Bake 9-12 minutes until browned. Cool for a minute or two on cookie sheet before removing with a spatula.

Preparation time: 20 minutes
Makes 2-3 dozen cookies

Tackle Herbed Chicken Stock

This nutritious stock can be used to cook rice, simmer vegetables, thin sauces and make super soups. I have used chicken breasts to make the stock because I like to remove the flavorful meat off the bone and use it in another dish like 110% Chicken Noodle Soup (page 54).

2 tablespoons olive oil
1 tablespoon butter
2 carrots, chopped in large chunks
2 stalks celery, chopped
1 leek, chopped
1 onion, chopped
1 turnip, chopped
2 teaspoons salt

3 quarts water
2 bay leaves
4 sprigs rosemary
4 sprigs marjoram
4 sprigs thyme
½ cup chopped parsley
½ lb. chicken breasts (or other parts)
1 tablespoon rice vinegar

Heat oil and butter in a large soup pot. Add carrots, celery, leek, onion, turnip, and salt. Sauté until all vegetables are soft and juicy. Add water, all herbs, chicken, and vinegar; bring to a low boil. Lower heat and simmer for 30-45 minutes. Allow to cool, remove breasts, strain stock into glass jars, and store in the refrigerator until needed. Meat from chicken can be removed, sliced, and used in soups, pasta, or rice dishes. Stock will keep at least a week.

Preparation time: 1 hour
Makes 3 quarts stock

Dribble and Shoot Quinoa

This grain (pronounced keen-wah) comes from the Andes Mountains in South America where it was once a staple food for the Incas. It has a delicious, light, nutty flavor and has the highest protein content of the whole grains.

1 cup quinoa
Pinch of sea salt
1¾ cups water

Rinse quinoa well with warm water and drain. Place rinsed quinoa, salt, and water in a pot. Bring to a boil, reduce heat to low, cover, and let simmer 15-20 minutes, until all the water is absorbed. Fluff with a fork before serving.

Preparation time: 20-25 minutes
Makes 2½-3 cups

Mental Focus Brown Rice

Rice is the principal food for one-half of the world's people. Rice with the hull, bran and germ removed is white rice. Rice with just the hull removed is brown rice. Brown rice comes in a variety of types. Short grain, long grain, and basmati are three. All of these varieties can be prepared according to the directions below.

1 cup brown rice
Pinch of sea salt
1¾-2 cups water

Rinse and drain rice. Place rice in a pot with salt and water. Bring to a boil. Turn heat down until rice is at a low simmer. Cover the pan and let simmer for 45-50 minutes or until all the water is absorbed. Don't stir the rice while it is cooking.

Preparation time: 55 minutes
Makes 2½-3 cups

Big Catch White Rice

Use white rice as a base for dishes like Man-to-Man Black Bean Stew (page 70), Crack of the Bat Vegetable Curry (page 76) or as the filling for Victorious Vegetable Sushi Rolls (pages 80-81).

2 cups white rice
3½ cups water
1 tablespoon butter
pinch of salt

Place rice in a bowl, cover with some water and wash rice for 5-10 seconds. Drain well. Bring 3 ½ cups water to a boil in a medium-sized pot. Add butter and salt. Add rice and return to a boil. Reduce heat to very low and simmer 15-20 minutes or until all of the water is absorbed.

Preparation time: 30 minutes
Makes 6 cups

Eye On the Ball Oatmeal

Whole grain oat groats that have been heated until soft and pressed flat are called rolled oats. Add a dash of brown sugar and a splash of milk to this hot cereal for an excellent pre-game breakfast.

> 1 cup rolled oats
> Pinch of sea salt
> 3 cups water
> ¼ cup raisins (optional)
> ½ teaspoon cinnamon (optional)

Place oats in a pot with salt and water. Bring to a boil, reduce heat, cover and let simmer on low for 20-25 minutes. Add raisins and cinnamon during the last 10 minutes of cooking if desired.

Preparation time: 25 minutes
Makes 2½-3 cups

Clean Pass Pressure-Cooked Beans

Chick-peas (garbanzos), pinto, black, lima, navy, kidney, great northern, Swedish brown, and cannellini are some favorite varieties of beans. Pressure cooking beans saves time, increases flavor and aids digestion. Today's pressure cookers have safety valves that prevent accidents.

2 cups dried beans, soaked 6-8 hours
4 cups water
Herbs and spices
1-2 teaspoons sea salt

Drain off soaking water. Put soaked beans and fresh water in pressure cooker. Add herbs or spices that will flatter the dish you are making (e.g., bay leaf, cumin, thyme, chipotle chili, ginger). Attach lid. Bring up to pressure on medium heat. You should hear a soft hissing sound. Lower heat and let beans cook 40-45 minutes. Remove from heat and allow pressure to come down naturally or run cold water over the top of the cooker. Add 1 teaspoon salt after cooking. Taste and add more salt if needed.

Preparation time: 45-50 minutes
6 cups cooked beans

Plant Your Feet Black-Eyed Peas

    1 cup black-eyed peas, soaked 6-8 hours
    2 sprigs fresh thyme
    1 bay leaf
    Juice of one orange plus water to make 1¾ cups liquid
    ½ teaspoon sea salt

Drain peas and place in large pot with herbs and liquid. Turn heat to high and bring up to boil. Lower heat slightly and simmer peas for 20-25 minutes, until tender. Remove from heat. Discard herbs, add salt to peas and mix gently.

Makes 2½-3 cups peas
Prep time: 25 minutes

Mix It Up Pancake Mix

It is nice to make a lot of this dry mix and keep it in a sealed container in the refrigerator or freezer. Economical too! The mix can turn into fabulous Flipturn Flapjacks (page 52) quick as a wink.

    3 cups unbleached white flour
    2 cups whole wheat pastry flour
    1 cup buckwheat flour
    3 tablespoons baking powder
    1 teaspoon cinnamon

Combine all ingredients and store in an airtight container.

Makes 6 cups dry mix
Preparation time: 10 minutes

Show Show Show Pesto Sauce

Grazie Mille to my friend Elena Leonard for her tried and true pesto recipe. Not just for pasta! Try spreading some on toasted bread and making an incredible sandwich with fresh mozzarella and fresh tomato. Whoa. Multiply the recipe as much as you like and freeze batches in 1-cup jars for quick, future pre-game meals!

2 cups tightly packed basil leaves (about 2 ounces)
½ cup extra-virgin olive oil
2 tablespoons pine nuts or walnuts
2 cloves garlic
½ teaspoon salt
½ cup freshly grated parmesan cheese

Before measuring, remove stems from basil leaves. Rinse and spin dry the basil. Blend first five ingredients together in a blender or food processor until smooth. At this point you may freeze the mix for future use in a clean jar or a plastic baggie. If using right away, stir the parmesan into the basil mixture, then stir the sauce into pasta that has just been cooked and drained. Serve immediately. To defrost frozen pesto, place in refrigerator for 8 hours, or put in a bowl of warm water for an hour or so.

Preparation time: 10 minutes
Makes about 1 cup (enough for 1 pound of pasta)

Resources

Gloria Averbuch and Ashley Michael Hammond. **Goal! The Ultimate Guide for Soccer Moms and Dads.** (Rodale Press, Emmaus, PA, 1999).

Sowell Jennings, M.S., R.D., Debbi and Suzanne Nelson Steen, D.Sc., R.D. **Play Hard Eat Right: *A Parents' Guide to Sports Nutrition for Children.*** (Chronimed Publishing, Minneapolis, MN, 1995).

http://www.gssiweb.com/ (free membership). Gatorade Sports Science Institute (GSSI) is a research and educational facility established in 1988 to share current information and expand knowledge on sports nutrition and exercise science that enhance the performance and well-being of athletes. The materials and services of the Institute are designed as educational tools for sports health professionals.

http://www.nal.usda.gov/fnic/ (no membership required). The Food and Nutrition Information Center is one of the most comprehensive nutrition web sites available, with a comprehensive list of nutrition topics/links, as well as a variety of nutrition tools such as nutrient composition, dietary assessment/analysis and energy calculators.

http://www.sportsci.org/ Sport Science: An interdisciplinary site for research on human physical performance. Click on "Sport Nutrition."

Index

For more great family recipes...

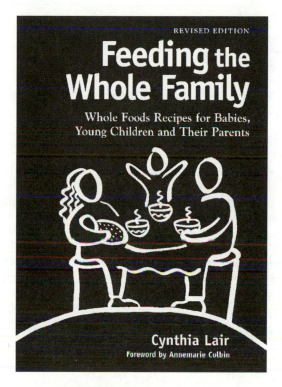

$18.00
288 pages; 7"x10"
fully illustrated; soft cover
ISBN 0-9660346-1-9

Over 25,000 copies sold.

- How to cook one delicious meal that will feed everyone – babies, children, and parents
- Over 150 family-tested recipes using whole grains, beans, vegetables, and fruit
- Insights on breastfeeding, starting solids, and whole foods cooking
- Special binding lies flat
- Index, glossary, and nutritional analysis of recipes

Reviews of Feeding the Whole Family

Finally, a cookbook that addresses the fact that no one has the time or inclination to cook separate meals... **Feeding the Whole Family** is full of nutritious, whole foods recipes that everyone will like.

L.A. Parent Magazine, March 1998

Feeding the Whole Family is the perfect guidebook for families interested in whole, organic, natural foods. Essential for those who want to start solids naturally without a big fuss.

Peggy O'Mara, *Mothering Magazine*

This book fills an important niche and will be treasured by the cook who wants to prepare delicious, healthful fare that the whole family can enjoy. It will likely remain among a family's favorite cookbooks long after the toddlers have reached their teens.

NAPRA ReView, Sept/Oct 1998

I have been feeding my family out of this book for a while and everything we have tried has been a success: fast, healthful, tasty, and appealing to children. This is just about the perfect cookbook.

New Beginnings, November/December 1999

This vibrant introduction to whole foods meal planning is full of tasty ideas. Ms. Lair has included recipes that are innovative and fresh ... a great book for the dad or mom who wants to make sure his or her family is eating healthy, and a really good guide to converting those fast-foodies into whole-foodies.

Vegetarian Journal, Nov/Dec 2000

This is a truly everyday useful cookbook. Cynthia Lair understands what it is like to cook for a family. She arranges the book so that you can cook for grown-ups and kids and not have to cook twice. One devoted carnivore friend said, 'Wow, you could make a paper bag taste good,' after he tasted the Tempeh Stroganoff dish I made from the book. I smiled but all the credit goes to Cynthia.

New Homemaker.com, May 2000

This is a book that says - relax - here's how to use whole foods and feed your family from the same pot ... each recipe includes a box on how to make slight adjustments for the little ones. You'll find common-sense support on how to eat when you're breast feeding, start your baby on solids, and make homemade baby food. I'll bet this cookbook won't end up sitting on your shelf.

A Real Life, June 1998

Latest Reviews of Feeding the Young Athlete

The book is concise, clear and practical. It is full of great tips to healthy, fuel-producing eating and simple explanations. Its true beauty, however, lies in the insidiously clever way it uses athletics performance to get kids to make lifelong changes in their diet.

Richard Seven, *Pacific Northwest Magazine*, January 2004

Being physically active requires wholesome eating. Authors Cynthia Lair and Scott Murdoch, PhD, RD explain how by following their sports nutrition guidelines, individual athletes and teams can find a whole new level of play. Eating wisely and well increases energy, endurance and the ability to concentrate and the authors provide recipes to enable families to achieve this.

Karen Newton, *Richmond Parents Monthly*, May 2003

Feeding the Young Athlete provides top-notch advice on why and how to feed your rising star.

Mothering Magazine, July 2003

With the increasing attention being paid to the problem of overweight Americans, this book assists players and their parents in finding and preparing the right food for healthy eating. This is a simple, easy to read book that gives suggestions for pre-game and post-game meals, explains hydration and provides "high performance" recipes (see recipe for Breakaway Banana Date Bread).

Robin Carroll, Minnesota Youth Soccer Association

...chock full of wonderful information and tasty recipes. Offers valuable information, useful charts - much more than your average cookbook. With titles such as "Man-to-Man Black Bean Stew," what young athlete could turn you away?

Dawn Dailidenas, *NW Baby & Child*, May 2003

Feeding the Young Athlete is easy to read. The section on what and when to feed the young athlete is excellent. For the parent looking to improve their player's nutrition, this could well be the book!

Kay Catlett, Executive Director, Ohio Youth Soccer, November 2002

Feeding the Young Athlete is a practical guide to help parents understand and apply the science of sports nutrition in the kitchen and on the practice field. The healthy recipes taste so good that my children have already picked out their favorites.

Susan M. Kleiner, PhD, RD, FACN, author of
Power Eating and High Performance Nutrition

ORDER FORM

_____ copies of *Feeding the Whole Family* at $18.00 $_____

_____ copies of *Feeding the Young Athlete* at $12.00 $_____

Special team rate 20% off!

_____ (10 or more) copies of
     Feeding the Young Athlete at $9.60 $ _____

                Shipping (see chart) $ _____

                Subtotal $ _____

                WA residents add 8.8% tax $ _____

                TOTAL $ _____

> ### Shipping & Handling Rates
> $3.00 per shipment plus $1.00 per book
> (for example: $5.00 shipping for 2 books)

Name _____

Street _____

City/State/Zip _____

I will be paying by: ❐ check ❐ credit card

Please make checks payable to **Moon Smile Press.**

Credit card type: ❐ VISA ❐ Mastercard

Card number: _____ Expiration Date: _____

Authorized signature: _____

Allow 7-10 days for delivery
Mail or fax this form to:

M O O N   S M I L E   P R E S S

11038 27th Ave. NE
Seattle, WA 98125

phone: 800-561-3039 fax: 206-365-1124
You may also order books at www.feedingfamily.com